C0-APX-274

THROUGH GRIEF'S
TENDER HEART

A literary embrace for the Grieving Heart

Through Grief's tender heart

Poems & Prose
to Soothe, Reflect, Guide & Inspire

JULIA DELANEY

© 2023 Julia Delaney

Julia Delaney, author
Title: Through Grief's Tender Heart

The contents of "Through Grief's Tender Heart" are for informational
and supportive purposes only and are not intended as a substitute
for the medical recommendations of physicians or other healthcare
providers. The information provided is to help readers cooperate with
professionals in their mutual quest for optimum well-being. Readers are
advised to review and understand the ideas presented and to seek the
advice of qualified professionals before undertaking any of the practices
or approaches suggested in this book.

All rights reserved. No part of this publication may be reproduced, dis-
tributed, or transmitted in any form or by any means, including photo-
copying, recording, or other electronic or mechanical methods, without
the prior written permission of the publisher, except in the case of brief
quotations embodied in critical reviews and certain other noncommer-
cial uses permitted by copyright law.

First Edition

ISBN: 979-8-9896595-3-1

Published by DIGroup
Printed in USA
Website: www.PositivePranic.com

CONTENTS

From Shattered To Sheltered   229

Grief's Deception 261

HERE WE ARE

So here we are, you and I, at the very beginning of this connection of ours. In your hands lies a journey that was once mine alone. This book, now translated into the words you read, began as a mosaic of emotions and experiences, shaped from scattered reflections written in moments of searching, healing, or of simply being in the presence of grief. Over the years, these writings were my silent partners, capturing the raw truth of my experiences as they unfolded.

Each poem, each story, each piece of prose originated from a place of deep personal need—a need to understand, to express, to connect with the parts of myself that I could only reach through words. They were not initially intended for others' eyes. Instead, they were conversations between me and my shifting shadows, written without the forethought that they would one day assemble into the chapters of this book.

Yet, the mere act of bringing these pieces together, of revisiting the emotions and insights they contained, became an unexpected healing journey in itself. It was a process of rediscovery, of seeing the transformation in my own life mirrored in the evolution of my writing. What started as a personal testament to my grief has blossomed into a shared narrative.

I offer these pieces to you now, not as a chronicler of grief, but as a fellow traveler well acquainted with its terrain. If you find within these pages a voice that echoes your own, a sentiment that speaks to your heart, or a moment of recognition, then my heart's work will have reached its fulfillment.

Thank you for being here, for allowing my past to intersect with your present. It is my sincere hope that the words I've compiled can offer you comfort, resonate with you deeply, and perhaps provide a measure of relief, recognition, or understanding in your own experiences of grief.

While grief is a solitary journey, we do not walk it alone. We share the universal language of loss, and in that, we find our most profound connections to one another.

With gratitude and warmth

Love, Julia

When love gives life, it brings along its twin;
In each heartbeat, grief is stitched within.
We love—We lose, in this revolving theme,
in each parting, Love gains a deeper seam.

INVITATION TO THE HEART

Here, in the quiet company of these pages, my heart unfolds before you. It's a silent offering, a gesture of kinship in the midst of our shared human journey. Each word, each memory laid bare, is a part of me reaching out to a part of you—perhaps the part that's searching for a voice, for a reflection, for a moment of understanding in the midst of loss.

This isn't just a sharing of stories; it's a sharing of soul. The laughter and tears, the quiet reflections, the sudden joys amidst the sorrows—all are threads from my life, now extended to you. They are an unspoken invitation to find, amidst these shared experiences, a sense of companionship, a whisper of comfort, a hint of recognition in your own journey.

In this space, we're not just author and reader; we're fellow travelers. My vulnerabilities, my strengths, my moments of insight—they're laid out for you, not just to observe, but to connect with, to find within them a resonance with your own life's path.

So, let's try to make sense of it together. We'll get into all the messy, confusing aspects of grief that often go unspoken, finding strength, understanding, and, just possibly, a touch of peace. Here, grief is not a shadow to be feared but a part of our collective experience to be acknowledged, embraced, and transformed.

As you move through this journey, let each page be a step closer, a deepening of our connection, an acknowledgment that while grief is personal, it also unites us in profound and unexpected ways.

One Grieving Heart

Do you want to know my story,
the way I've grieved unborn and taken,
dreams shattered,
hopes deceived,
secrets concealed,
abandoned and forsaken,
love's trust unretrieved,
wounds ever unhealed,
paths untraveled,
a heart forever aggrieved?

Should I tell of friendships lost in time's cruel tide,
or promises broken in trust's painful divide?
Speak of passions cooled, or dreams cast aside?
Each is a tear in the fabric where sorrows hide...

What of opportunities missed, or paths not taken,
regrets that linger, haunting, unawakened?
Or the silence in a room, where laughter once rang,
the void left behind,
a glimpse of what's lost,
a soul's pang?

Perhaps you know the ache of a goal unrealized,
or the sting of rejection, harsh and undisguised.
The loneliness in crowds, a disconnect so deep,
a word unsaid, or secrets that weep?

But as I wander through these memories and thoughts,
a realization dawns, clear and unadorned.
There's only one story - raw, sincere, and wise,
the story of a Grieving Heart in the landscape of Life.

Because if we love, we grieve, it's life's refrain;
Without Love, Grief's essence we can't explain.
The more we love, the more we bleed and heal,
but in the heart of it all, there's a truth we feel.

It's one narrative,
one human,
one soulful chart,
a story not of many but of One Grieving Heart.
A connection we share,
a language we all know,
a bond that transcends life's intricate flow.

So here's my tale,
not mine alone but ours,
a reflection of human essence,
of life's fleeting hours.
Through pain and joy, we wander,
we impart,
this universal story...
the tale of One Grieving Heart.

When a part of you feels buried with lost dreams,
healing sprouts from the deepest wounds...
from within.

May you be cradled by the compassionate hands
of time, gently guiding you through healing.

JULIA DELANEY

NO INTRODUCTION

There's no introduction,
no forecast,
there's no guidebook,
no beginner's course,
no rehearsal for this unyielding force.

Just a chair unused,
a cold cup of tea,
the silence where your laughter used to be.
Unannounced,
grief claims its space,
in the everyday it traces your face.

Dropped into a sea of sorrow, wide,
no lifeboat,
no place to hide.
no need for words,
no comforting lies,
just the aching truth in my cries.

But in this void, I find a sign,
a pulse of Love, enduring time.
No warning for this sudden twist,
Yet in the silence,
Love persists.

INTO THE SILENCE
OF
BROKEN BONDS

...grief needs no script,
no guide,
no expectation,
it bridges every divide,
it's raw,
it's painful,
a storm within the soul,
a tumultuous ride, often out of control...

STITCHES IN SILENCE

Here I am, again, trying to pick up the pieces of a shattered dream... Do you know that feeling? The one where you've stitched your future into the very fabric of someone's being, and then, they're gone. Just like that... One minute they're there, your heart fluttering at their mere presence; the next minute, they're not. Their abrupt exit from your life leaves you clutching at the thin air where they used to be, leaving behind the haunting emptiness of what was supposed to be your shared future. It's a future that's now shattered pieces of your puzzle, your dream, and each piece feels sharp enough to slice through your tender heart, rattling your sense of reality.

A veil of fear descends, and the sharp edges of loss, sadness, and incompleteness begin to dig deeper. You know, it's like having a fortress you've built brick by brick, each one a cherished memory, a shared laughter, a whispered promise, and then standing there, helplessly watching it crumble to dust. It's a tough spot, and it's okay if you're still figuring it out. I still am, for sure...

When the dream you nurtured so dearly disintegrates, it almost feels as if a part of you has been buried alongside it. Grief, in its very essence, feels like an intimate death, a silent funeral for the part of our identity that we nurtured through our bond with the one who is no longer here.

The Muted Ache

The mind, staggered by the shattering of dreams, instinctively reaches for anything that might soften the blow. It's like being in a wild ocean of sadness and confusion, trying to construct a life raft from whatever debris you can find. But in reality, quick fixes, distractions, rushed attempts to "get over it" are merely stopgaps. Through the lens of my years and the losses I've weathered, I've learned that it's not about scrambling for an instant solution but rather about giving grief the time and space it needs to unfold naturally. It's about waiting, about allowing grief to weave its story within you at its own pace. And it's in this waiting, in this quiet unfolding, where healing finds room to breathe.

When we're grappling with the heartbreak of losing a loved one, a child, a parent, or even a beloved pet, we often plunge into the icy void of grief. In our desperation to escape the bone-chilling cold of loss, we may hastily try to fill the vacuum left behind. Maybe we rush into a new relationship, or swiftly welcome a new baby, adopt another pet, or seek parental affection in others, all in an attempt to restore what was lost. But by doing so, we're building these new bonds on the quaking sands of unresolved grief, denying ourselves the chance to let our sorrow flow naturally, to rise and recede in its own rhythm, giving us the healing and acceptance we need.

Grief is a profoundly personal thing, you know. We all experience it in our own way, and there's no universal guidebook to navigate it. No roadmap, no instruction manual.

When that deep, gnawing sadness envelops me, I've learned to lean into it, gently... Ever so gently, like you're easing into a warm bath. And while there, I remind myself that healing takes time. It's as if there's a silent clock inside each of us, ticking away at its own pace, as we try to find our way in a world that feels different now.

And that's the heart of it—there's no rush. Just like no two people are alike, our paths through grief aren't either. We each have our own way, and it's filled with peaks and valleys, twists and turns; it's not just a straight line from start to finish. We're all just doing our best to find our footing, stumbling along at our own pace, in our own unique and beautifully human way.

Beneath the Quiet

As the sand in the hourglass keeps falling, the sharp sting of grief slowly starts to dull, turning into a quiet hum in the backdrop of the heart. The sharp shards of shattered dreams start to smoothen out, and gradually, little by little, you find yourself stepping into a new rhythm of life. It's a delicate dance, this journey...

Life... Life is often compared to a road trip, right? We like to think we've got it all figured out, that we're in control of the ride. We assure ourselves that we know what's coming up next; we can handle the next loop, the next plunge. But can we ever really predict what's ahead? Maybe it's more about finding peace in unexpected moments amidst the unpredictable twists, accepting the process rather than trying to control the ride.

Sometimes, there's a gentle pause in the sorrow, a tiny island in the sea of grief where you find yourself feeling a bit lighter, maybe even healing... It's like a single soft ray of sunshine piercing through heavy clouds.

But then, unexpectedly, a familiar wave washes over you. An old piece of clothing, a smell, a tucked-away keepsake, a certain sound—the simplest things can reopen the floodgates. And suddenly, you're swept back into the vast ocean of grief. Yet, when the tides of loss pull you back under, let a gentle whisper remind you: "It's okay". It's okay to grieve, to remember, to let your feelings flow. It's all a part of the process...

Once a Dream Was Mine...

Once a dream was mine,
I held it firm in my hand,
woven tight with expectations,
a future so grand...
Then, torn from my grasp, the dream did fall,
plummeting like a stone in a well,
echoing loss
like a lonely,
hollow
bell.

The urge to avoid, to run, to hide in a new space,
neglecting grief's path,
its erratic, winding pace;
building on the sand, where tears freely poured,
ignoring the healing,
the heart's whispered word...

I've learned that grief needs no script, no guide,
no expectation, it bridges every divide,
it's raw, it's painful, a storm within the soul,
a tumultuous ride, often out of control.

Yet, in its wake, healing begins,
inner strength stirs a new life within;
a timid rhythm that gently sways,
a new existence in the light of day.

Kissed by a Ray

Today, I woke up,
kissed by a ray of sun
gently on my forehead...

I caught my breath,
creeping out from the night,
shaking off dreams heavy like lead...

Tears welled up,
a release from dread,
dropping onto life's delicate thread as jewels,
each a precious reminder of the miracles that
dawn brings,
an unspoken gratitude
that quiet morning reveals...

Barefoot,
I tread into the backyard...
a warming brew comforts my hands...
the morning sun, my tender lover,
its golden kisses too grand...

Venturing deeper into the shadowed garden,
under the trees' grandstand,
Life stirs within my heart,
calling to expand.

In the warm palm of my hand, a secret I hold—
a tiny, unassuming miracle,
a seed of a kind unknown.
I cradle it with tender zeal,
feeling the pulse of its life's dormant rhythm...
An inclusive expansion longs to be unsealed.

In my sorrow, I cradle a seed with hope,
swirling it like a grain of sand,
knowing that it's not an ending,
but a chance for life to make demand.

Just a speck, yet a sparkle,
mighty seed holding life's command,
releasing pain, not forgotten,
but fertile in this land.

In the heart of the earth,
darkness tenderly holds my hand,
nurturing growth,
where once only grief dared to stand.

Each day is a gift,
each moment is life,
beautifully unplanned
in this infinite moment of being,
I am...

I have no words to soothe your pain.
All I can offer is a space in my heart for you.

THE UNSEEN BIND

Grief... Grief has a way of sneaking up on us, catching us off guard when we least expect it. It can be overwhelming, and at times, it feels like we're walking through a thick fog, unsure of where to turn. It's easy to feel isolated, lost, and alone in the midst of such pain.

Do you know what helps me? I just close my eyes and think about all the people out there who are going through tough times, just like me. I can feel their pain through my own, and as my heart expands with that pain, I know I'm not alone... I try to send them some comfort, love, and support through my thoughts; and do you know what? It actually helps me. It really does.

The beauty of being human is that we have the ability to connect with one another, to lean on each other during difficult times. In the face of grief, we can find solace in shared experiences and the understanding of others.

When Words Fail

In your pain, my words falter,
as if tripping over their own inadequacy,
I search, I rummage through the language,
yet, no word feels enough, no phrase sufficient.

I wish I could reach out,
pluck a star from the night sky to light your path,
gather the sun's warmth to soothe your chilled heart,
but all I have,
all I can humbly offer,
just a warm, quiet space in my heart.

It's not a grand gesture,
no fireworks, no grand orchestra,
just a quiet room filled with soft light,
a warm corner,
an open chair,
a silent invitation to simply be,
be you,
here,
now...

This space,
it's here for your sorrow,
for your unshed tears,
for your sighs,
for the words caught in your throat,
for the memories that sting and bite,

for the laughter that's lost its way,
for the immense love unexpressed,
pulsating with a longing to burst, to release,
trembling at the seams of silence,
desperate to be free...

And in this quiet space, you are welcome,
welcome to grieve,
to rage,
to remember,
to laugh,
to weep,
to whisper their name,
or to sit in silence,
in the echo of what was,
knowing it's heard,
it's held,
it's honored....

There are no expectations here,
no timetable for your grief,
no 'shoulds' or 'musts',
just the promise of a presence,
the steadiness of a heartbeat echoing your own.

And so, in my silent offering,
I hope you find a gentle comfort,
a space where your pain
doesn't need to shrink or hide,

where it is seen,
understood,
embraced,
in the safety of this shared silence,
in the depth of the warm heart,
where you know,
you're not alone,
we're all connected in Love.

Because even when words fail us,
when they crumble under the weight of the
pain,
we have this,
this shared space,
this quiet understanding,
this resilient bond of shared humanity,
where even in grief,
you are home.

In Moments of Despair

In moments of despair, when I feel so alone,
I close my eyes, my heartache like a heavy stone,
and imagine others, their pain much like my own,
together we share a bond that's rarely shown.

In the darkness our struggles intertwine,
our hearts beat together, yours and mine,
feeling the weight of pain that's shared,
in this agony I find solace in a moment spared.

I reach out with thoughts, a gentle embrace,
offering comfort and love in a warm heart space,
to all who suffer right now, just like me...
and in the heart of compassion, I find a way to be free.

Because in the midst of sorrow, when all seems lost,
our shared pain builds bridges, connections embossed,
and by giving support to others, I extend and expand,
I discover the warmest, kindest part of myself,
and my heart starts to mend...

Just Like You

positivepranic.com/JustLikeYou

This guided meditation helps us feel more connected and less alone.

STRENGTH BENEATH THE RUBBLE

You know, when it felt like my world was crumbling around me, I had to muster the courage within me to start sifting through the emotional wreckage, looking for the hidden joy beneath all the rubble.

One of the things I had to do was allow myself to feel everything, to let my emotions pour out unfiltered. Honestly, this was one of the most challenging things I ever did. Some days, I'd find myself crying until everything felt numb, letting the hot tears release a bit of my pain. Other times, a memory would gently bubble up, lifting the corners of my mouth into a tender smile, reminding me of happiness in its purest form.

There were days when rage would erupt from nowhere, a fierce and fiery beast gnawing at my insides. And then, there were times when I felt a strange calm would wash over me, like a serene lake on a still morning. Emotions I didn't even know I was capable of feeling rose to the surface – a tumultuous blend of sadness, anger, nostalgia, and even a flicker of hope.

On some lonely nights, I'd be overcome with longing for what once was, my heart aching under the unbearable weight. How can you miss someone so deeply, so intensely, that it feels as if a silent scream is building up inside you, threatening to shatter your existence into a million pieces?!... And then, as if out of nowhere, gratitude would sneak up on me during quiet moments, reminding me of the love and warmth I had experienced.

It felt like I was caught in a whirlwind of emotions, my heartstrings being tugged in every direction. But I realized that embracing these feelings, rather than pushing them away, was a crucial part of my healing process. Each tear, each laugh, each sigh was a step forward on my way to rediscovery.

So I allowed myself to feel without judgment, to express my emotions in their rawest form. And through this process, I began to see the glimmers of happiness that had been quietly waiting for me all along.

The Courage to Feel
or Letter To Self

Hi there, my dear,
I know it's not easy for you
to be here
now,
where words lost all meaning,
but when they say:
"just be strong" or "all will be fine"
you get upset,
and your chest gets tight.
You just want to scream and cry,
but your eyes remain dry...

Words don't make you feel better.
In fact, they may hurt.
So I wish I could hug you from miles away
and through time I would fly
to get rid of your pain.

I understand,
it feels like the world is filled with dust,
so you can't see far enough
to allow yourself to go and to trust,
and the breathing is tough,
and whenever you look,
you can't see the light,
you can't find the goodness, it seems...

But I plea you to try and to trust it is here,
and you know what you know,
and you hear what you hear...
you remember that light and darkness,
with highs and lows,
are a natural process of life for us all,
we all go through this once in a while,
so I hear you,
and I feel your heart as it beats right here,
inside mine.

And there is no need to understand
or make sense of it now,
but please know,
 it will end soon.

One morning
you'll wake up,
and you'll see the sun -
the sun that shines just for you,
and you'll hear little birds all around
singing a beautiful song
just for you,
and you'll feel
how the tender breeze caresses your skin
as if you're the most cherished being in the
world;
and you'll feel
you're Alive and well,
striving to Live and see the joy in each day.

And as you rise,
in every little thing you do and touch,
you'll embrace a new way to stride;
and you'll see
that all the darkest moments of your life
made you a wiser, deeper,
more compassionate and loving being,
so you can be there
for every living-breathing thing...

But for now,
I just ask you to hope for the best,
and never give up,
knowing the light will be back.

This time of your life might be here for a reason
or not,
but I promise,
you'll look back on it knowing
that you're all right,
and that
it's okay to feel sad right now;
it's allowed.

Pour your heart on the paper,
or sing a song,
curl up under a blanket and let your tears flow,
be alone if you have to,
dance like mad if you want,
do whatever you need to,

but deep down,
remember
that this is a stage,
and the main actor
is
you;

and that this is your story,
your life,
and your tears,
you're in charge of it all.
So let the tears flow as you write it your way,
the way you want it to go;

I believe you can do it,
you're amazing and strong,
you get brighter and wiser,
in the experience,
you grow.

Uncharted Core

Peeling away my hardened shell,
where silent secrets often dwell...
To feel it all,
the heart's unfiltered core, a daunting task,
like mapping an uncharted shore;
tears traced paths till all sensations fray,
purging pain,
releasing anguish away...

Yet, within the hollow sound of sorrow's tide,
bubbled up sweet memories, gentle in their glide,
lifting corners of my lips in a tender, knowing dance,
mirroring happiness, in its purest stance...

Unexpected, rage ripped through, a fierce fiery beast,
its claws shredding composure, its roar disrupting peace,
burning bridges within, it left ashes in its wake,
a testament of turmoil, a path of heartbreak...

In the wake of anger's relentless burn,
I find calm... a welcome return,
a range of emotions, diverse and vast,
a complex portrait of my past.

Some nights, I'm engulfed by a longing so vast,
lost in the aching remnants of a deep-rooted past...
But somehow, gratitude finds its way,
a reminder of love's warm ray.

Caught in the wild currents of my heart's tide,
through highs and lows, I glide.
Every tear—a silent testament to sorrow's bite;
Every laugh—a spark in the night;

In each sigh released, a part of me unfolds,
marking my progress as the story is told without judgment,
revealing a show stripped of pretense,
a heart's truth in its most intense.

Then, a subtle clarity came into sight,
revealing the dormant joy patiently waiting for the light.

In this freedom to feel,
to openly face raw, unrefined, uncharted core,
hidden deep within,
in the most vulnerable place of the unguarded space,
I found my healing,
my strength,
my unguarded grace.

Searing

"Just sit with it," they say,
a chorus faint and worn,
But do they know?
Have they felt this searing inside?
This agony, this storm, that leaves the spirit torn,
a tempest wild, where peace and solace cannot abide.

In the cacophony of life, where laughter rings hollow,
and joy's light dims, overshadowed by loss's veil,
I stand,
a vessel of pain,
too vast,
too deep to follow,
adrift in a sea of betrayal,
where hope seems frail.

JULIA DELANEY

IN THE HEART

OF

HURT

I embrace my feelings,
each one as a whole,
because healing begins
when I honor my soul.

MELDING WOUNDS

Letting ourselves feel what we feel when we're hurting...
it's tough, isn't it? For me, it's a big part of learning to navigate
those darker times. There's no magic formula, no 'right' way
to grieve, but I find that honoring my feelings, sitting with
the pain does something important—it helps.

Grief can be a lonely place. Sometimes it feels as if you're
the only one in the world feeling this way. But it's not just
you or me. There are many of us, each trying to make sense
of their own heartache. You know, there's something oddly
comforting about that, knowing we're part of this larger hu-
man experience...

You know how a simple thought, a kind word, can mean
the world when you're hurting. By offering love and support,
even just in my thoughts, I find solace in the act of extending
compassion beyond myself. It's as if understanding is a bridge,
connecting our experiences.

Walking through grief can feel like stumbling in the dark, but somewhere along the way, we might discover a strength we didn't know we had. We learn that we can endure, that we can find our way back into the light. There's growth there, in the pain and the sadness, a chance to understand others, and to lend a hand. And as we're moving through, there's comfort in knowing we are in this together; that in the midst of it all, you're not alone.

In quiet moments, when we pause to take a deep breath, we might find a small measure of comfort and peace. It's in these fleeting moments that you can begin to heal and see once again that life, in all its complexity, is still beautiful and worth living.

Breathe...

Here...

Now...

Through Grief's Tender Heart

When sorrow holds me in its cold embrace,
it seems as though joy has left without a trace;
But deep within, a warm flicker of light persists,
patiently waiting to be rekindled amidst life's twists.

In the darkest moments, I find my way,
through grief and loss to acceptance, a path I lay.

Through tears and heartache, I learn to grow,
embracing the pain, letting Love overflow.
Even in sorrow, I find moments of grace,
as I cherish a glimmer of light within,
in this ever-changing inner space...

Together we'll talk, just like friends often do,
sharing from the depth of our hearts,
both the old and the new.
I embrace my feelings, each one as a whole,
because healing begins when I honor my soul.

Acceptance is a challenge, but with an open heart,
I know I can find strength and courage, a fresh start;
Though my world has shifted, Love still remains
in joy's smallest moments—my happiness gains.

Pain, carving trenches deep
in the bedrock of my being,
within these cavernous depths,
my true self starts freeing.

Howling Heartbeats

Grief... It felt like awakening to a world robbed of its hues, the bright colors replaced with a grayscale palette. You know how it feels when someone we love leaves us, it's like losing a part of yourself. We invest so much of our hopes and dreams in those we hold dear; and when they're gone, we're left with a void that feels insurmountable.

I've trodden down that path, and at times it feels like navigating terrifying terrain. It's not just about being sad or upset, you know; it feels like a piece of your identity has been scraped away. When your life is so entwined with the ones you love, their absence can feel like a personal demise.

So, grief... It's the mind in a relentless tug-of-war with this abrupt transition, struggling to reconcile with a life that suddenly feels distorted. Some days, the sorrow would engulf me, and it felt like my heart was howling...

Grief... Grief operates on its own clock.

I know... it's tough... Yet, surrendering to the tidal wave of grief, experiencing it in all its rawness, that's an essential piece of the healing puzzle. It's about extending patience to yourself, embracing your pain, and allowing it to light your path through these challenging times.

It's okay to feel hurt. It's okay to grieve, to feel the void left by what once was. Your heart is far more resilient than you give it credit for. Believe in its strength, in your strength. You'll navigate your way through this, just as I did (and still do)...

Ripped by the Current

Beneath the guise of a gilded sunrise,
there lies a force, unseen, unkind,
a rip current, silent and treacherous,
an abduction of the soul, not the body confined.

Each sun-kissed wave—a seductive lie,
that masks the undercurrent's cold embrace,
my heart is a ship wrecked in this raging storm,
lost in the tempest of time and space.

Oh, the ocean, to your depths, my pleas rebound,
a pit of despair—in your swirl I'm found.
The sun above—an indifferent round.
My unheard scream is the only sound.

Ripped by the current, a phantom pain,
a cherished one, snatched away, unseen.
The echo of laughter, the memory of touch,
forever imprinted in life's unfolding scene.

Alone I stand on the shore,
peering into the abyss,
my heart is an open sore.
Each breaking wave is a fading sigh of a life
that's here no more.

My bare feet are etched by grains of regret,
my tears are mere droplets in this endless sea.

The breath of the shore
and the kisses of the tide
are reminders of the love that was
and will forever be.

In the relentless pull of the undercurrent,
in its icy grip,
in its merciless sweep,
the shards of my heart I clutch,
in a world that no longer seems mine to keep.

Yet within this agony, a glimmer persists,
a flickering flame untouched by the heartless current,
a testament to unknown strength in the depths of my
despair,
        where I discovered me
witnessing the rage of the current in its ruthless blow,
I am a mother,
a lover,
a warrior,
a grieving girl—
haplessly watching a cherished one
ripped by the current's cruel bow.

In the face of sorrow,
I'm brought to my knees,
yet still I breathe...

A Bond Unbroken

I weave a tender thread
with tears and whispered prayers,
walking the edge of sorrow's sea
where hope and darkness blend.

My eyes, like stars that light the night
in search of you, my dear.
Through fields of shadow, pain, and fright
my love will never veer.

And in the deep quiet of my soul
some strength begins to stir...
The fearless Love,
a timeless Whole,
our fates forever blur.

I gaze at night in search of solace sweet.
My dear, twinkle in the sky,
two deep, sweet, wounded hearts,
someday again we'll melt
I know...

Oh, Love that stretches vast-and-wide,
a boundless endless grace,
a bond unbroken,
side by side,
in every tear that's traced.

Breath of Solace

Treat yourself with kindness and care,
you're not alone on this road we share;
Give yourself love like you would to a dear friend
and watch as your wounds begin slowly to mend.

Take a moment to breathe,
feel the air in your chest...
in this simple act
you might find solace and rest.

As the sun gently rises,
a new day begins to bloom,
through the darkness of grief,
life's beauty resumes...

THE WOUNDED WISDOM

Pain, the uninvited guest, often shows up at our doorstep in the darkest hours, bringing with it a cascade of emotions, a tornado of despair. Its presence is unwelcome, its message is seemingly destructive. But within its harsh whispers, there lies hidden a sage's wisdom, a teacher's lesson.

Pain.... I want it to go away, yet I understand that pain, in its purest form, is not a malevolent enemy, but a mirror reflecting back to me parts of myself that need care and healing. It nudges me, pulls me, sometimes even drags me into the deepest recesses of my being. It forces me to confront my vulnerabilities, my fears, my past, my reality...

When pain's knock echoes through the hallways of our existence, we have a choice. We can try to drown its calls in distractions, or we can bravely open the door, face it, let it in, sit with it, listen to it... And this is no easy task; it demands courage, resilience, patience. But in this daring act of embracing, in this profound acceptance, we have a chance to find the seeds of transformation.

The heartache that once felt unbearable starts to morph into strength within you; the grief that seemed everlasting becomes a wellspring of compassion. The shattered pieces of your soul start to form a mosaic of courage, wisdom, and love. You rise not despite your pain but because of it.

As we step into the light, unburdened yet stronger, we might even realize that pain wasn't an adversary but an ally. It was the chisel that sculpted us, the fire that tempered us, the darkness that made us long for the light. In its stark reality, pain carves deep, yet it's in these hollows that we often find our depth, our humanity, our true self.

And just like that, you move forward... forever changed, ever-growing. Pain has etched its story in your heart, but it is you who holds the pen. We carry with us not just the memory of our suffering, but the knowledge of our strength, the proof of our resilience, and the promise of new beginnings.

Life is a dance, they say, and pain is a step within. It is a heavy step, but one that shapes us in ways no joy ever could.

So, I dance, weaving through my pain, spinning with my growth, twirling towards a destination unknown. With every beat, with every breath, I am more... I am alive... I am human...

When Pain Slinks In

At midnight's edge,
pain slinks in,
an unexpected guest,
uninvited, unasked,
it settles in my chest...
Not a demon,
nor a villain in the silent night,
instead—a brutal teacher,
shrouded in moonlight.

Pain is a mirror,
unforgiving,
revealing all I've lost,
dragging me relentlessly,
no matter what the cost,
pulling me into darkened corners
where my secrets lie,
where truth with fear and memory,
in tangled shadows tie.

Pain knocks,
a steady rhythm, reverberating loud,
and I'm left with a choice under its thundercloud:
do I drown its relentless drumming,
or let its truth seep in?
An act of courage,
a challenge where transformation might begin...

Heartache,
once a gaping wound, morphs into a scar;
Tears,
once a salty tide, now a northern star.
Broken bits of me assemble in a new design,
a testament of endurance,
of strength that's truly mine.

I rise,
not despite,
but because of this aching pain—
the artist of my soul,
a masterpiece in making,
in its ruthless honesty,
pain sculpts, carves, creates,
within this raw and hollowed space,
my true self resonates...

With the dawn,
I step into the light,
with a load that's lighter,
carrying not just my scars,
but the grace of acceptance...
and in this light I see
Pain,
my daunting adversary,
now an unlikely guide;
its story is written on my skin,
but I am the one
who holds the pen within.

Life is a dance,
pain a step within,
heavy yet profound,
shaping me in ways that joy could never surround.

And so I dance on,
twirling with pain,
spinning with growth, not in vain,
in each ticking second,
with every pulsing beat,
with every fleeting breath,
I imbibe life's ceaselessly vivid,
palpable
heat.

I was handed a night sky void of stars,
a cloak of heavy sorrow.

It took the patient unfolding of time,
to see the dawn of tomorrow.

How Much Pain Can One Heart Take?

How much pain can one heart hold
between the beats, untold?
Does it quantify in sighs that slip,
or in silent tears from the eye's tip?

Is it a quiet lake, deep and vast,
mirroring ripples of a shadowed past?
A tome filled with grief-stricken moments spent?
Is there a limit or is it infinite?

Does it measure in the whispers of the night
when all that's left is the moon's cold light?
Or the ache that lingers in laughter's wake?
How much, indeed, can one heart take?

The heart, a field of love and pain,
a scene of loss and love again...
Does it swell with the sorrow it has known,
or is it softened by love that's grown?

Is it etched on the soul, a deeper wound
in places unseen, in silence, it's shrouded and tuned?
A vessel of longing, carrying sighs' old tides...
Does it live in the moment when a dream dies?

How much can one heart bear and still endure,
through each sorrow, each painful cure?

Does it shatter, does it break, or merely bend
in its quest for a beginning or an end?

Yet, within this fragile vessel, so worn,
lie seeds of hope that in resilience born.
How much pain can one heart embrace
and still pulse with love, and grace?

In each question a story unfolds,
of a heart that's brave and bold.

How much pain can one heart take?
As much as the endless waves in a lake.

It's in the question, we truly find
the strength of the heart,
a glimmer of light in the darkest night.

It's not in the pain but the courage to shine.
In this brave question we find the divine...

The heart, much like a boundless lake,
in its depths, Life's melody awakes.
With every wave, with every twirl,
unfold stories of facing the world.

BOUNDLESS BEATS

How much pain can one heart take?—Asking that question, it's like staring into a mirror that reflects back my own raw, vulnerable self. It's real, isn't it? Life dishes out its share of bumps and bruises. But what's astounding is not the pain itself, it's our ability to take it, process it, and then get back up.

We all know pain; it's as human as breathing. The sting of rejection, the hollowness of loss, or the harsh slap of failed dreams—it all sinks down into the heart, finding a home there. Our hearts, they're where we hold our love and our pain. But more than that, they're the place where within each heartbeat, we find the strength to understand that every stumble, every fall, doesn't spell the end. It's just a different beginning, a chance to pick ourselves up, dust off, and start anew, fortified by the experiences that brought us to our knees.

We're not built with a limited capacity for pain. We're not cups that overflow when we've had too much. Our hearts are more like a lake, depth unknown, expanding with every ripple of hardship. Every sigh of disappointment, every tear we try to hide, it doesn't crack the heart, it broadens it, enlarges its ability to hold and heal.

You might think all this pain would make you hard, toughen you up. But that's not what has to happen, is it? We don't have to turn into stones. We might soften. We might open up to other human experiences and pain. Our hearts learn the language of empathy, of understanding. We might start seeing our reflection in others. That's resilience; that's strength. It's transforming not despite pain but because of it.

And here's the other side of the coin—with pain comes love. Love and hope are the constant companions to our suffering, weaving through our stories, and adding color to our existence. Even in the midst of throbbing pain, the heart remembers to love, to hope. It knows, without darkness, there is no light.

What makes us strong isn't that we don't feel pain. It's that we feel it and acknowledge it; and when we cry: "How much can one heart take?" It's in that moment, in that question, that we can tap into something no less than divine. It's the kind of courage that has seen us through centuries, through wars and famines, losses and wins. It's the strength of humanity, the strength of a boundless heart.

So, life will throw its punches, and we'll feel the pain. But the thing is, the heart takes it, holds it, transforms it, and learns from it. So, how much pain can one heart take? The answer is not a measure, but a promise—a promise of enduring, of growing, of loving. Because hearts, they're made to beat and to brave, they're made to bear and to hold, and above all, they're made to love.

Depth Unseen

There's a living lake within each chest,
its depths unknown, where secrets rest.
It's not a cup, its brim has no edge,
it's like a pulsing ocean with no ledge.

Each setback stirs the silence, deep
in shadows where the moonlight weeps.
Its expanse grows wider, yet ever serene,
with every twilight met by dawn, its depth unseen.

In this hidden lake, we all bear.
Each sorrow drowned, morphs into prayer.
Each secret sob, each silent scream,
feeds this lake, stirs its dream,
yet never broken, but emboldened and vast,
a symphony boundless, a limitless cast.

The mirrored surface of this living lake,
reflects who I am now and who I'll make.
Pain is not a tempest but a shaping tide,
carving bigger hollows for Love to reside.

Gently rippling under stormy skies,
This pulsing lake is full of life.
Daring to swell, a tale to tell
of Love, resilience, courage, and strive.

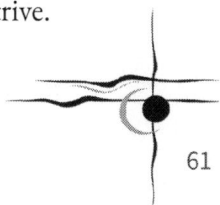

Lilies... they were sitting right on the side table,
filling a room with their essence, when my little
JoJo took her last breath...
Lilies...
Lilies... she smelled...

A Scent Of the Last Breath

Lilies bloom with a promise—
a vow whispered to still air,
yet their fragrance stifles,
a heavy blanket in a room too small for their scent.

Tiny feet, minuscule boundless heart—
your absence fills rooms,
breaks all barriers,
eclipses the sun.

A choice too immense
crushes down on a chest already tight.
Who am I to snuff a candle
that once outshone the moon and stars' light?

Your snout twitches—
is it the scent of what lies beyond
or a betrayal, perplexing
as the lilies' essence that lingers around?

Forgiveness I plea,
a prayer I can't quite voice—
yet, in the whispering leaves, in the morning sun,
I search for your silent choice,
for your soul unbound...

In the soil under the tender young tree,
your frame takes root.

May your essence unfold
In a place unburdened by questions too profound.

I kneel before the tender tree,
Lilies' petals trailing my tears, kissing freshly turned soil.
Oh, please, hear my soul weep for you in prayer—
know I love you,
please forgive me,
set us both free...

THE WEIGHT WE CARRY

Yoking Existence

You know, there's an object called a 'yoke,' usually made of wood, that you've probably seen in old movies or historical documentaries. It's that thing that gets placed over the necks of two oxen, linking them together so they can pull a heavy plow or cart. Seems like a relic of a bygone era, doesn't it? Just a simple, agricultural tool... That yoke is more than a chunk of wood; to me, it's a pretty deep metaphor for life's burdens and bonds. When seen through the lens of grief and loss, it becomes a physical manifestation of an emotional and ethical commitment we make to another being—animal, human, or otherwise.

The yoke isn't merely about physical labor, sustenance, or survival. You're not just pulling a shared weight; you're navigating the landscape of shared experiences, emotions, and, ultimately, shared existence. In fact, if you've ever heard of yoga, the word itself comes from the same root, it's derived from the Sanskrit root 'Yuj', meaning 'to yoke' or 'to unite.'

In this spiritual union, the yoke is not a burden but a symbol of connection—not just to another being, but to the universal spirit that threads through all of life. I feel that in the intimacy of shared burdens, there's a doorway to something transcendent.

Caring and Giving

When it comes to caregiving, you're thrown into a whirl-pool of gut-wrenching choices. I'm talking about the kinds of choices that keep you up at night. Like, do you give more pain meds, even if it clouds their awareness, just to see them comfortable? Or do you hold off because you want one more coherent conversation? When the doctors throw stats and survival rates at you, do you listen? Or do you hold tight to what you know the person really wants? These choices, they're not checkboxes on a form. They're soul-searching, heart-ripping moments where you're asked to peek into the divine, into the raw core of life and love itself.

Through the act of caregiving, through the immeasurable weight of the choices we must make, we're offered a deep look into the sacred essence. Not a god cloaked in the grandeur of mythology, but a quiet divinity that can be found in the raw moments when love confronts loss.

So, this yoke I'm talking about isn't just physical; it's emo-tional, spiritual—ties that connect us to each other and to something far greater than ourselves.

Grief has its own language, one that defies the neat bound-aries of words, flowing into the spaces where logic fails. When you carry a yoke—whether it's made of wood, or love, or an intricate blend of soul fibers—you carry a potential for both love and loss, the likes of which can reshape your entire being.

When that yoke is removed, either by choice or by cruel, uninvited circumstance, you don't merely lay it down; you feel as if a part of your soul has been hollowed out. The yoke is no longer there, but the weight is—in your chest, your shoulders, the pit of your stomach. It remains, an absence so palpable it's as if you've lost an essential part of your own body. Suddenly, your hands are empty but your heart is unbearably full, full of love that has no physical place to go.

In the grieving process, this yoke takes on new forms. It becomes the early-morning ache, the midday emptiness, the nighttime longing. Here, the yoke transforms—it becomes a loom, each thread a memory, each shuttle-pass a day in a world forever changed yet still turning. This loom weaves unanswered questions into its fabric, each an echoing chamber in your heart: 'Could I have done more? Could I have loved better?' These questions don't seek answers; they seek a reckoning with the incomprehensible nature of loss.

The yoke in its physical absence becomes a spiritual presence, a connection you feel to a being who's no longer by your side. It's an almost mystical tether that links you to what you've lost, and paradoxically, to all that you still hold within. You feel that responsibility never ends; it merely transforms. Now, you're responsible for remembering, for honoring, for carrying the essence of the lost one within you, in the actions you take and the love you extend to others.

In grieving, you're pulling a plow through soil that's both barren and fertile—barren because of the physical absence, yet fertile with the emotional growth and spiritual presence that come from the ache of love, untamed and unpossessed.

The Unseen Bridge

Grief's yoke can be haunting, but in its spectral weight, there's a form of grace, an unexpected lightness. It's as if in carrying this invisible burden, you gain access to a new emotional aspect, one where love isn't erased but transmuted into a new form of relating, and not just to those who are no longer with us, but to ourselves and the often inexplicable world around.

In carrying this yoke of grief, you don't move away from the one you've lost; you move closer, immersing into the universal experience of being human. The weight of the yoke, then, is both a burden and a bridge. It ties us to the earth even as it elevates our understanding of what it means to be human—or beyond human. To carry it is to recognize our role as participants in a much larger, more mysterious dance of life and death, union and separation, love and loss. It can be heavy. Yet, it's a weight that, when shared in love, has the power to elevate us to new realms of understanding and connection—both earthly and divine.

It's not about 'moving on' or 'getting over,' nor is it about transcending or forgetting. It's about carrying forward, about navigating a world that's forever altered but still filled with opportunities for renewal and compassionate connection.

The yoke you carry in grief is a poignant reminder that Love, in its most authentic form, doesn't know the bounds of physical existence. It's a gravitational pull from the soul of the world to the heart of the being.

Sometimes, the weight of the decisions we make for those we love most feels unbearable, as if we've crushed something irretrievable and beautiful.

Yoke

In a room drowning in tears,
beside a chair, a vase—
Lilies smell too damn strong,
like the choice I wish I didn't have to make.

JoJo—tiny feet, sweetest heart, boundless soul,
you filled gaps I didn't know I had,
making my fractured life
feel somehow whole.

Sixteen years, you've been my light,
through darkened rooms of my own making,
your blind eyes saw me—
and my fractured world you were remaking.

Years spent navigating silent darkness,
sweetheart, you became my eyes—
while I held your fragile body,
you guided me to see my own disguise.

Your care a ceaseless ritual—
endless lifts and cleansing, plates and pills—
yet it's your agony, a wail of your relentless pain—
that's a weight on my soul I couldn't quell.

Steroids, narcotics, antibiotics—a perpetual wheel,
your ears a traitorous soaring silent field,
yet your tenacious spirit could never kneel.

71

You stayed ever sweet,
sleeping snuggled in your sling,
on my belly,
at peace—complete.

In your final chapter, wracked with pain,
I faced a choice where each option a loss—
to hold onto you a moment more,
or free you, no matter the cost.

I wished for nature to decide,
to take you softly, on her tide.
Instead, it was my voice that shook—
it was my hand that took.

Doctor's shots—one, two, three,
your little body stilled on my knee.
A cry escaped your lips, a plea—
Did you feel my love?
Could it set you free?

And in that heart-wrenching moment,
as you wailed your last, unknowing cry,
I hope you felt my love surrounding you,
as I howled a soul-ripping goodbye.

My arms a cradle,
for hours holding tight,
as your essence faded,
into the depth of incoming night.

The lilies stared, their scent a cloak,
as if they knew the heaviness of the yoke.

Now, under a tree, your form takes its rest—
Love's all I have left,
untamed and unpossessed.
Forgive me, sweetheart, for playing God—
for the choice I've made, for this painful part—
I hope you roam in boundless presence,
joyful and free.
Yet, questions linger,
heavy as the lilies-scented night —
could I have loved you better,
in darkness and in light?

Your ears closed, but your soul open wide,
now free from all earthly strife—
I long for your forgiving whispers,
on the other side of this earthly life.

In the restless pursuit of meaning, I often found myself caught in the unyielding cyclone of existence, racing toward the horizon, chasing dreams that felt just beyond my grasp. Yet, in the swirl of this endless quest, I'd often overlook subtle whispers of wisdom—gentle nudges suggesting that maybe the treasure we seek isn't tucked away in some distant realm but right here, woven into the very fabric of our existence.

I wrote the following poem to commemorate an amazing experience that happened the day after I was diagnosed with cancer. This poem is my testament to the boundless beauty that unfolds when we accept and surrender to what is—to the present moment.

You can take it as an invitation to step away from the ceaseless cacophony of thoughts and to immerse in the quietude that exists at the very core of your being.

Unbound

Unexpected and pure a moment unveiled,
all identities stripped of me, as my world got derailed;

With open eyes I witnessed my self dissolve,
all were there in its shining glory—
but my body no more...

In the realm of the senses, I was unbound,
lost in the beauty of life's vibrant sound,
time's tether slipped,
in that moment, I melded as one
with the breeze and the trees,
and the warm morning sun.

No past or future, but only the now,
a seamless connection so deep and profound,
all barriers melted in a dance so divine...
I was one with creation
immersed in the sublime.

Rooted and present—no ground beneath,
I felt the universal Love as a tender wreath all around me,
I saw the intricate weave
of life's vivid fabric, a wonder to conceive...

No pursuit, no seeking, just the grace,
born of suffering my heart had to embrace;

It opened up the moment,
an eternal dance,
a world unveiled a sight profound,
within life's breadth,
boundless Love was found.

In Twilight's Dance

When silence rules and heart is touched by pain,
I search for peace in life's relentless gale.
The world may splinter, yet a spark remains,
piercing the gray as joy regains,
beyond despair, a glimmer guides my way.

In twilight's dance, both joy and sorrow twine
like ancient friends,
a testament to Life.

You know,
when the sun through clouded skies does shine,
where joy and sorrow meet,
there, at this point,
Life thrives.

And in this fleeting moment, small and unadorned,
a laugh, a scent, a warm embrace restored,
in this simplicity, the bliss is born;
Each simple joy - a universe to behold.

Embracing pain,
I let memories' hold fade away,
knowing that from the depths of darkness
the sun will rise again.

In the ache of being—a whisper,
strength stirs, raw and real, growing crisper;
Bared to love, to grief, the world's rough embrace,
an unshielded heart finds its own sacred pace.

UNSHIELDED HEARTS

Inside each one of us, there's a quiet kind of strength. Even when life gets messy, this strength doesn't fade away—it actually gains volume. It turns into something like a personal anthem, especially in the midst of hardship. It's a common thread, a pulse of grit that runs through all of us, gently pushing us to keep going, to find a way to rise, no matter what life brings.

Life often seems complicated, right? It throws fear, doubt, and so many unknowns our way. But amidst all these ups and downs, we can discover our genuine selves, our authentic voices, and our untapped strength. We often guard our hearts as if they're behind a high-security wall, shutting ourselves off from all the incredible experiences that might very well be waiting for us out there. But when we let those walls come down, even just a little, we start to see life in high-def—every color, every emotion, as real as it gets.

Being present in life, truly feeling the highs and lows, perceiving and absorbing each shade of joy and sorrow—that's bravery, that's courage. It empowers us to engage deeply, form meaningful connections, and better understand ourselves and others. It turns life from a daily grind into something much more—it paves the path to accepting our wholeness and harvests freedom born from genuine comprehension.

And the next thing you know—it's not just about surviving or drifting through life anymore. It becomes more about diving into the deep end, exploring joy and sorrow, and examining what makes us who we are. We learn to mindfully embrace life, taking each experience as a thread in the ever-changing fabric of who we are, choosing to be fully Here and to make the most of Now. When we dare to live this way, we're not merely surviving; we're actively shaping our lives, transcending survival to truly thrive.

I know that when I close my heart in fear, when I shut down emotionally, I lock myself away from the beauty and love that surrounds us. But when I dare to bear, to be vulnerable, to stay open, to really feel both joy and sorrow—that's when I find the courage and strength to live and love, to connect deeply, and to be truly free.

Dare to Thrive

With an open heart, I can dare
to face the pain and to bear the glare
of all the hurt, doubts, and fears
that try to hold me back through years;

And in that bearing,
in that choice,
I gain a strength,
a new-found voice
to Live and Love,
to truly Be,
connected,
whole,
and fully free.

Yet, when we close our hearts in fear,
we lock ourselves away, unclear
of all the beauty that surrounds
and all the love that can be found.

So I let my heart break and shatter
again and again,
moment by moment,
I allow it to flutter...
because in the breaking I'm fully alive,
in pain, I found the will to thrive.

And though sometimes it's tough,
I know that an open heart is enough
to face the truth and the reality of life,
with all its joys and pains
there's not much lost but only gained.

Because, in the bearing of the unbearable,
I've found my strength,
my will to live,
my need to strive,
accept,
move on,
and be,
my courage,
my ultimate Love,
and my will to give.

Now, again, at this very moment, I'm opening my heart, continuing to dare to bear, and to dare to thrive, finding the courage and strength to keep going.

Because in the end, that's what matters—the will to thrive, to accept, to move on, and to be. And that's what gives me the courage to face the truth, the reality of life, and to live it to the fullest.

ACCEPTING

LOSS

In brambles barefoot through pain, I tread,
a wrestle with change, where paths may lead;
A heart both torn and whole, I find,
a life reshaped, with grief entwined.

BAREFOOT THROUGH BRAMBLES

In one of the most daunting challenges I've ever faced, accepting my loss, there were moments when I'd awaken in the morning, expecting to find the world as it once was. But as the hazy edges of dreams receded, the stark contours of my altered reality seeped in. I had to grapple with the undeniable truth that things had irreversibly changed. Swallowing this bitter pill was heart-wrenching – there was no turning back, no magic wand to restore what was lost. This profound change had cast a long shadow over my life, a constant reminder of a deviated path, leaving me wandering in unfamiliar territory.

In the depth of that realization, I found myself tangled in the thorny brambles of denial, bargaining, helplessness, despair, anger, and regret. I kept questioning and pleading endlessly. I replayed moments over and over, like a helpless moth drawn to the flame of 'what if'. The relentless surge of change was an ever-present force. Each day felt like a battle, a fight against the current of change, a struggle to accept the new normal, to reconcile with the unfamiliar landscape of my life.

Finding myself in the thick of denial, I felt like I was chatting with my own echo in an empty room. The constant sound of 'why' ricocheted off the walls of my thoughts. It was as if I were a traveler with a map of a place that no longer existed, fumbling to find my footing on unfamiliar terrain. That 'why' was a backpack filled with bricks, and I felt like I had no choice but to carry it.

Then came the bargaining... It was a bit like trying to haggle at a market stall where the seller is utterly unmoved. I found myself trying to trade the peaceful present for a few moments of the past. The irony is that life is the strictest of shopkeepers. It wouldn't let me swap today's calm for yesterday's storm.

And boy, the despair... Despair felt like standing at the edge of a cliff with a blindfold on. I couldn't see the bottom, but I knew it was there. My heart felt hollow, with every beat echoing into its emptiness. It's like standing in a fierce wind, exposed, all alone, with nothing but your loss swirling around you like fallen leaves. That's how I felt...

As for all those cherished moments, they kept playing like old home movies. Sweet moments of laughter and love were now silent films that only I could see. And regret... that sneaky thing; it started knitting a scarf of 'what could have been,' every knot is a painful reminder of a different ending that never happened.

At times, I was ensnared by Helplessness... the Helplessness... It felt like being adrift in the open sea—vast and overwhelming, its depths unfathomable. No land in sight, the horizon a blurred line where my hopes seemed to dissolve. My heart beat like a feeble ripple in the vast silence, each pulse a futile signal seeking solace, a tender plea for comfort, lost to the uncaring winds. This immense expanse became my home for a while, a dwelling of despair, where I floated, weightless yet burdened, on this boundless expanse, my only companion being the relentless tide of my emotions. My emotions.... they rose and fell, the undercurrent of sorrow threatening to pull me under... into its depths, a silent abyss of grief...

And the Anger... It felt like having a volcanic core, a fiery tumult just beneath my surface, endlessly churning. No warning of the eruption, only the inevitability of its explosive force. My heart, hot and ablaze, each throb a potential spark setting my world on fire. It was like standing alone on a volcanic crest, scorched rocks of regret tumbling around me. The fury within me seemed to manifest as molten emotions, flowing, searing, reshaping the landscape of my soul. That's how Anger consumed me...

All I can say is that every day felt like a tug of war with change. Waking up was like stepping into the boxing ring, and each night was just catching a breath before the next round. This new 'normal' was like learning a new dance, one where I had to move to the rhythm of resilience.

But you know, in all of this, I figured that accepting what had happened wasn't some finish line I had to cross. It was more like taking a long walk on a winding path. Each step was a chat with my inner self, and every breath felt like a hand-shake agreement with acceptance. And you know, I walked this path not because I was brave, but because I didn't have any other road to take. This path I tread not out of courage, but necessity – the only way forward.

Once I started embracing this reality, something shifted within me. I noticed the morning sun rays dancing on my skin, the symphony of birds chirping outside my window, the comforting warmth of a cup of tea. I realized my life had indeed changed, but my capacity for love and happiness was still there, untouched, perhaps even expanded by the depth of my grief.

That's when I understood that it was okay to grieve and, at the same time, find joy in the little things life had to offer. It was okay to miss what was while appreciating what is. It was okay to cry for the past and smile for the present. Grief didn't have to be an all-consuming darkness; it could coexist with the light. And so, even amidst the raw void of my loss, I found pockets of happiness hidden in everyday moments, waiting to be discovered.

Denial

In the quiet breath of dawn, I'm awake...
an actor on a stage,
reality at stake.
I walked the tightrope of 'as it was,'
the spotlight of truth paused on 'because'.

Shadows danced in my echoing room—
a dance of 'why' in resounding gloom.
My footsteps treading on yesterday's map,
fumbling in the heart of a memory's lap.

Stooped under questions, a backpack of stones,
through corridors of the past, amidst silenced tones,
reality knocked, yet I chose the blind,
in the fortress of denial, a self-imposed bind...

My heart mirrored an abandoned hall,
echoing 'why', a resounding call.
On the playbook of yesterday, my mind insisted,
against the tide of truth, that my heart resisted.

Wearing denial like a cloaked mask,
hiding in the comforts of the past,
like a child with fingers in my ears,
I drowned out the chorus of mounting fears.

But the drumbeat of reality, steady and clear,
played its rhythm for all to hear.

I danced with denial, swaying and spinning,
in the silent dance of unending beginning.

Yet, beneath the whispers and the shouts,
the seed of truth began to sprout.
Even cloaked in the comfort of denial's song,
I knew the tune wouldn't play for long.

Volcano's Heart

Anger erupts, no polite knock on the door,
roaring from the heart's molten core.
No sweet lullaby, no gentle dance,
just the electric pulse of a lightning bolt.

Loud as thunder, wild as a storm,
defying the norm, refusing to conform.
In the void—echoes of what's undone,
an explosion of questions with the rising sun,
the world moves on, indifferent, aloof,
and I'm here,
barefoot on the roof,
screaming at the stars,
fists to the sky,
demanding answers from the silent night.

Anger – a raging fire, a burning tide,
a raw confession I cannot hide.
No saint, no sinner, no laurel, no blame,
just a raw nerve in the frame of the game.

Mirror on fire,
reflecting despair,
a smoky veil in the open air.
In its red glare, I'm exposed,
my love,
my loss,
my wounds disclosed.

No pretty poetry,
no rhythm or rhyme,
just a heartache
burning in real-time,
in the furnace of Anger,
in its fierce light,
I'm laid bare,
stripped of polite.

Anger is no villain,
no demon to shun,
just a heart under the scorching sun.
Beneath its heat—a Love profound,
in its throbbing beat,
I am unbound.

In the untamed landscape of my grief,
Anger is raw, unfiltered relief.
In its fiery grip,
I dare confess
the depth of my Love,
no more,
no less.

The Invasive Vine

Guilt – a twisted root, burrowing deep, slighted,
a parasite feasting, leaving the heart benighted.
Woven in the shadows, it spreads its unseen lace,
a creeping vine, binding memories in a cold embrace.

In the quiet hours, it rises like a tide,
its accusatory whispers are impossible to hide.
An onslaught of moments, like shards of broken glass,
each a cruel reflection of an irrevocable trespass.

Guilt's sickly sweet poison, pervading every thought,
in the web of should have—could have ought.
Its grip, relentless, like winter's icy hand,
a cruel puppeteer, pulling unseen strands.

The replay of footfalls in a desolate hall,
an unending loop, a spectral call.
Like ink in water, it taints every scene,
an insatiable beast, voracious and keen.

Yet within its torment, a raw and painful birth,
a mirror held to the complex weave of my worth.
In its harsh light, the outlines of Love appear,
etched in the silence of a falling tear.

In grieving, fear doesn't appear as a distant threat or a philosophical conundrum. It's more like an untamed heartbeat—a rhythm felt but not seen, deeply unsettling yet so fundamental to our very essence.

This fear isn't the enemy in a tale of "you against the world"; it's more like a pulse that, despite its deep discomfort, keeps us grounded in our humanity, our vulnerability, and the enduring strength that lives within each of us.

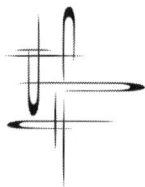

In the hollows of absence,
in the chill of the void,
there beats a rhythm, cold and stark—
the pulse of fear,
relentless and unswayed,
a rhythm that knows my name.

THE COLD PULSE OF FEAR

Fear in grief is not a shadowy figure lurking in the corner of a room—it is the room itself, the walls that close in, the floor that gives way beneath your feet. It's the dissonance in the silence that follows a loved one's laughter, now forever stilled. It's the vacant chair at the dinner table, the unspoken words that hang heavy in the air.

This fear is not fleeting or abstract. It's tangible, a persistent reminder of a world turned inside out, a life fractured into before and after. It's the panic that seizes you when you reach for the phone to share a trivial moment, only to remember that the person on the other end is not available to you.

The fear in grief is the terror of forgetting—the sound of their voice, the warmth of their touch, the way they looked when they were lost in thought. It's the crushing realization that memories, once so vivid and alive, can fade into the fog of time.

It's the fear of living, too. Living without them, living with the void they've left, living with the unrelenting truth that life goes on, indifferent to your loss. It's the mundane terror of stumbling upon an old photo or a note scribbled in their handwriting, and feeling time collapse, bringing the pain of loss rushing back; of cooking for one less, of figuring out how to fill the hours that were once occupied with shared joy and routine.

And then, there's the fear of oneself. The fear of what this grief has made you, the stranger in the mirror who wears your face but carries in their eyes a pain you don't recognize. It's the fear of never healing, of being forever defined by this loss, of becoming a monument to a love that once was.

But there is another profound fear in grief - the fear of betrayal. The fear that moving on, finding joy again, loving again, is a disservice to the one who is no longer around. It's the guilt that gnaws at you when you catch yourself smiling, the shame that creeps in when you realize you've gone an hour, a day, a week without crying. This fear is not a singular emotion; it's a spectrum, a complex, ever-shifting landscape that I navigate without a map. It's a journey without a destination, a process without a clear path.

In grief, fear is both a barrier and a companion. It isolates me, even as it connects me to others who have known loss. It's the raw, unvarnished truth of being human, the cost of loving deeply and fully.

In grief, I see fear as not something to be overcome or vanquished. It's something to be lived, to be felt in all its terrifying, honest, and heartbreaking complexity. It's a testament to the depth of love that preceded it, a love that continues to echo in the chambers of a heart learning to beat anew..

In fear's dark maze, a way is found,
though twisted, rough, and all unbound,
the human heart, resilient still,
finds strength in pain, in loss, in will.

In the Jaws

Gripped in the jaws of a terror unnamed,
a heart pounds wild, unsteady, untamed,
the void of loss looms—a chasm unbridged,
Grief's icy fingers clutch, grip, and impinge.

A scream unheard, a cry that's silent,
Fear's dance erratic, mad, defiant,
eyes wide open in the dead of night,
a soul unraveled, lost in fright.

Unfamiliar rooms, a life unspooled,
the void shouts loud, chaos unruled,
each tick of the clock a thunderous roar,
time's march relentless, a never-ending sore.

What once was warmth is now jagged ice,
memories twisted—love's cruel price,
Fear's teeth gnash,
its breath a storm,
a mind besieged,
a spirit torn.

No calming words,
no gentle touch
can mute the scream of loss's clutch,
a world unhinged,
a path unclear,
the gaping wound of grief's raw fear.

Panic's pulse,
a frantic beat,
a life undone,
a soul's defeat,
Yet somewhere deep, a spark persists,
a hope,
a dream,
life's tenderest kiss.

Untangling

Why do I question, why do I reel,
in this whirlwind of emotions, so surreal?
Did I pull these strings?
Did I choose this fate?
Or is it just life playing out on its checkmate?

I hear the whispers, those cunning tales,
that it's all my fault, while my spirit quails...
But I need to pause,
I need to see,
that life's strokes of fate are not always 'me'.

This process of untangling isn't swift or smooth,
but in its twists and turns, I find my groove.
I learn to speak to myself in soothing tones,
like a friend in need,
not as mere bones and stones.

When all around me seems to fall apart,
the healing balm is my own gentle heart.
It's not about fixing what's perceived as broken,
but finding peace in words unspoken.

It can be a lengthy road, separating ourselves from the harsh whispers of self-condemnation.

Be kind to yourself; extend the same compassion and understanding to yourself as you would to a beloved friend. Because when the world feels like it's in fragments, self-compassion can act as a gentle glue, piecing together the shards of our broken normal.

Despair: The Unseen Chasm

My heart pounds in this vast emptiness,
each beat a hollow drum,
a spectral rhythm sounding the depths,
an anthem of the numb.

I stand on the brink,
blindfolded in despair,
unsure of the depth below,
unseen it remains,
yet its presence casts a shadow.

The wind that once whispered,
now strips away my guise,
my loss takes form,
swirling around like frigid winters' fallen skies.

All that was familiar,
all that I thought was mine,
now dances in the storm,
as I stand alone,
in this whirlwind, life has spun,
worn and torn...

A horizon of emptiness stretches before me,
a loneliness that devours,
a desolate landscape painted with silence,
beneath a sky that cowers.

Submerged in a sea of sorrow,
I drift,
an island with no shore,
in the vast depths of despair,
with no glimpse of before.

My heart,
it trembles,
each beat a hollow tale,
a rhythmic dirge of despair,
against life's gale.

I reach out,
seeking something,
anything,
to anchor my flight,
but all I find is the icy touch of the endless
night.

The quiet is overpowering,
each whisper a shout,
a concert of loneliness,
a chorus of doubt.

The world spins on,
oblivious,
while I remain,
still,
lost in the wilderness of despair,
caught in time's chill.

Despair is more than a feeling,
it's a lingering twilight,
a realm where the sparks of hope are masked,
hidden from sight.

But even in this darkness,
there's a sliver of light,
a glimmer of endurance,
preparing to ignite.

When despair floods in,
like the night consuming the day,
I realize,
in this stillness,
Life continues its play.

The pulse of my heart,
though faint,
still keeps the beat,
a testament of resilience,
in the face of defeat.

Moving Through Crowds

In dreams, I move through crowds
brimming with laughter, wrapped in clouds.
Yet inside, a gnawing silence takes hold,
a story in my heart, untold.

My light dances, vibrant and real,
a ray of warmth, they all can feel.
Yet beneath,
in the depths, unseen,
lies a heart that weeps.

Eyes meet mine, but fail to see,
the depth beneath, the silent plea.
A smile, sincere as the day,
yet the longing in my eyes they turn away.

On the surface—a joyous dance,
Inside—a longing for a deeper glance,
for communion,
for shared silence, for a gaze that knows,
for a moment of understanding,
as a gentle river flows.

I am their sun, yet I long for the moon,
the silent notes of an unsung tune.
In the heart of the crowd, I stand,
yet the song of my silence, they don't understand.

My pain is like a river running deep,
in my heart, secrets I quietly keep.
Lonely in the crowd, unspoken words unwind,
an untraveled path, left behind.

Yet, in this solitude, I hold a key,
to the locked door of my mystery.
In the silence, in the depth, in the unmet gaze,
I meet my honest, raw, unadorned space.

In the crowd
I am alone,
a single star, yet to be known.
In the silence,
in my heart's honest plea,
I am whole,
I am free.

So, I wear my solitude as a crown,
in the crowd, yet not worn down.
In my loneliness,
a lighthouse in the night,
a lonely star,
but burning bright with infinite light.

In the aftermath of loss,
my heart's relentless refrain,
Life's sweetest music composed in my pain.

The rhythm of Grief,
a sorrow so pure,
shaping the Love that forever endures.

Less

Helpless,
my heart—a faint ripple across the vast liquid expanse,
each beat—a fragile call,
a plea swallowed by the uncaring wind.

Unmoored.
                    Unanchored.
Drifting, floating,
                    landless, less certainty.
In this watery limbo, my temporary home,
where the horizon blurs into a fading promise.

My emotions,
                    rising and falling,
a tide that's both mine and more than me,
threatening to pull me under,
into the fathomless depth of a grief too profound.

Light yet heavy, I float.
This sea of despair - home for now,
home to a heart feeling less and less,
caught in the unending sorrow's tide mess.

Less.
In this less, I start to see more...
More surrender,
                    more acceptance,
                        more oneness.

With every less,
I merge with the sea of more,
I am less,
yet in this less I am so much more.

One with the ocean,
its rhythm now my own,
in the vastness, in the uncertainty,
I find hidden currents of unknown strength,
hopelessly helpless, yet powerful,
in this vast liquid expanse.

A Thief of Joy

Resentment,
a creature of the mind,
invisible to others, but oh so unkind.
At first, it seems harmless and small,
but it grows and festers, consuming us whole.

It enters our body like a thief in the night,
and slowly but surely, it steals our light,
we become its captives, its prisoners, its slaves,
and with each passing moment,
we're digging our own graves.

We hold onto it tightly, like to a precious stone,
as if our pain and suffering will be atoned.
But it's a delusion, a trick of the mind,
because all it does is make us bitter and blind.

It feeds on our anger, our hurt, our pain,
and it grows stronger, like a parasite in our brain,
it consumes us until we can't see
the beauty of life, the love, the harmony.

But we have a choice to let it go,
to release ourselves from its endless woe,
we can choose forgiveness,
letting love in,
and watch as resentment fades
from within...

Because in the end it's just an illusion,
a product of our fears mixed with confusion,
we can choose to be free,
to be whole,
and let go of resentment,
connect our souls...

Bargaining

In the stillness of the moment my heart begins to wander,
to the loud, bustling market of the past, it starts to ponder.
Trading today's tranquility for the storm of Before,
in this soundless dance, I find myself once more.

Through the labyrinth of time, I drift, reaching out,
holding onto fragments of past, dispelling doubt.
I offer my peace at the counter, hoping for an exchange,
for a few stolen moments within memory's range.

Each fragment of the past in my hands I hold,
seeking solace in its story, a tale to be told.

A distant laughter, a quiet song, a touch that's now gone,
in this marketplace of fleeting moments, my longing is drawn.
Old voices surface,
familiar silhouettes take stage,
a collage of smiles and faces begins to engage...

The past feels safe—a break from today.
But no matter how hard I try, the Now won't go away.

Life is tough, doesn't give an inch,
I ask for a break and don't get a hint.
The Present, it insists, is the only thing I own,
amidst the remnants of the past it stands, but not alone.

115

In my longing for what was,
the Now felt underrated,
yet, in its soft consistency,
it holds what's truly weighted.

Bargaining:
a futile negotiation in the marketplace of time,
a fruitless barter
for the timeworn song of a weathered chime.

It takes the marketplace of fading imprints
to truly conceive,
that the present, not the past,
is the actual reprieve.

So, in this market where the past is sold,
where memories get traded, bought, and told,
I step outside,
breathe deep,
and then I see—
the Here and Now
is where I'm meant to be.

Soothing Whispers
Lullaby for a Sorrowed Heart

In the still of despair,
hear my whisper soft and slow,
through the darkness and the tumult,
let these soothing currents flow.

In the hush of my words,
let your heart weave its nest,
feel the rhythm, the tenderness,
in the warmth of my heart,
find your needed rest.

A sound, nurturing, and tender,
a soft, whispered song;
in this melody of comfort,
may your rest belong.

The pain that used to grip you,
a torment fierce and wild,
yet, listen to my whisper,
gently as a child:

"I see you in your struggle,
I feel your aching soul,
In the silence of your sorrow,
you are not alone, you are whole."
Let the calm seep in,
embracing it with every cell of your being,

let it cradle you in its gentle fold,
with the sound of solace,
let warmth unfold.

In this quiet moment,
hear the harmony we weave,
in the softness of this lullaby,
let healing be received.

Your tender heart, it pulses,
beats in a rhythm of Love,
brave and ceaseless little drum,
even in despair, it won't succumb.

Vibrating with resilience,
it sings your truth so clear,
a lullaby of courage,
a melody so dear.

Each beat is softly spoken,
each pulse, a quiet might,
holding onto this moment,
a glimmer in the night.

Embrace the rhythm
feel the comforting warmth,
let the soothing words seep in,
you're not alone, my dear,
you're not alone,
I'm here and tranquility is within.

Life weaves its blanket,
soft threads intertwine,
both dark and bright,
in the pattern of your being,
every thread holds light.

So, rest your eyes, sweetheart,
feel my soothing touch,
you are seen,
you are heard,
you are cherished,
I'm here to share your pain,
it's not too much.

Feel the caress of my words,
let them sing you to sleep,
in the music of their whispers,
let healing seep.

Tomorrow will dawn anew,
a fresh page yet to write,
but now you flow,
flow through the depth of night,
softly into the morning light.

In the quiet of this moment,
with the whisper of this rhyme,
feel the soothing energy,
healing in its prime.

Each word a gentle caress,
each phrase a loving sign,
embrace the peace that's offered,
in your own sweet time.

Rest easy now, dear heart,
for as long as you need,
know that in every moment,
love continues to seed.

So rest in this quiet,
under the moon's tender light,
cradled in Love's rhythm,
and feel your spirit take flight

Lost

Lost, I am
in the stark vacancy of the mirror,
a chilling echo of laughter that's no longer there,
my eyes—strangers to their own form,
I am lost—
in a smile, that has turned into a grim of despair.

Broken,
the rhythm of us,
with words of love swallowed in silence,
a fog thickens, weaving uncertainties,
I am lost—
in the void of a monologue fading into ether.

Lingering...
in your absence,
once filled with touch, now an aching void,
arm's reach away, yet spanning galaxies,
I am lost—
in the hollow echo of a still-beating heart.

Hollow,
the laughter,
chasing your joy's shadow,
a desperate pursuit,
mirth replaced by quiet sighs,
I am lost—
in the raw memory of a last goodbye.

Vanished,
the joy,
life, once in full bloom, now banished,
sunrise to moon's crescent,
every phase of light and darkness,
I feel lost—
without the essence of you.

Lost, I am—
in the longing,
the grief,
in the ceaseless search for relief.

Yet, within this mournful song,
a testament of love stands ever strong,
even in the dense fog of sorrow's host,
In Love,
I discover—
I am never truly lost.

In hearts and dreams, a silence spread,
echoes of the words unsaid;
A longing for the touch, now lost,
regret's cruel dance, the grievous cost.

IN ECHOES OF THE UNFULFILLED

As for all those cherished moments, they became ghostly replays in the theatre of my mind. Each memory was like an old home movie; a silent, black-and-white film devoid of the joyous sounds that once filled them. The echoes of laughter and words of love were quieted, leaving me the only spectator to these mute reels of past joy.

Regret, that cunning trickster, with its needle-sharp sting, began weaving an intricate web of 'what could have been.' Each spun round was a testament of missed opportunities, a chronicle of choices made and actions not taken. Each delicate thread was a cruel reminder—a taunt of a different ending that never came to be.

Regret, the cruel puppet master, tugged at the strings of my heart, conducting a symphony of sorrow. It played on my vulnerabilities, twisted my memories, painting vibrant scenes of joy with the somber shades of 'if only' and 'what if.'

I found myself in an endless maze, chased by the specter of regret. Each turn, each corner—a harsh reminder of moments lost, words unsaid, and love unexpressed. Every decision, every action was scrutinized, magnified under the cold light of hindsight, and I was left longing for the warmth of ignorance.

As if the wounds of loss weren't painful enough, regret salted them with the haunting possibilities of a past rewritten, a present repurposed, and a future reimagined. It teased with the illusion of control, the mirage of a time machine, the seductive allure of second chances. But the only reality was the ticking clock, the relentless march of time, and the echoing emptiness where those precious moments once lived.

Regret held up a distorted mirror, refracting not what was, but what could have been, casting long, bleak shadows that danced mockingly over the relics of my past. The reflection was harsh, the reality colder, a bitter concoction of past decisions and present consequences.

But amidst the ruins, I learned. I understood the futility of wrestling with the past, of bargaining with time already spent. Regret was a deceptive storyteller, spinning narratives of 'might have been' from strands of reality. And I was its captive audience, bound in the chains of yesterday, torn between the past that was and the future that never could be.

Regret is the echo of choices made in the chambers of the past. It's the whispering wind that stirs the dust of forgotten dreams, the silent symphony of unfulfilled desires. But even in its cruel jest, it holds a lesson—a reminder that every moment counts, that every word matters, that every action, no matter how small, alters the course of our lives. The pain of regret is the price we pay for the wisdom it imparts.

Regret, You Silent Sculptor

Regret, you silent sculptor,
carving valleys in my soul,
each stroke a hollow trace
of opportunities untold.

You work in quiet moments,
twisting memories into mirth,
etching 'what if' and 'if only'
on the canvas of my worth.

Every stroke, a phantom future,
each etch, a chance unwon,
you sketch the unseen landscapes,
underneath the setting sun.

You toy with tender heartstrings,
pulled taut with heavy sighs,
replaying missed moments,
in the theater of my eyes.

Regret, you sly artist,
your palette full of pain,
the colors of 'might have been'
dancing in my brain.

You're a relentless chiseler,
each missed stroke makes me see,
how different the sculpture,
the masterpiece could be.

But despite your constant carving,
your etching and your mock,
I found my firm stand in the present,
against the ticking clock.

Though you may shape my sorrow,
you may trace my tears,
but you're not the architect,
of my remaining years.

Regret, you silent sculptor,
I see your craft, your art
but while you shape my past,
I'll sculpt my own heart.

And so, we dance, a dance eternal,
two sculptors in a play,
one shaping what has been,
one forming the new day.

Where Sorrow Slept

In the depths where sorrow slept,
an unspoken promise was quietly kept.
Tucked between what was and will be,
a morsel of acceptance started to unfold to me...

There was no finish line to cross,
no victory to declare, no coin to toss.
Instead, a quiet walk, no end in sight,
through twilight whispers of the night.

Acceptance wasn't a grand reveal,
but a gentle unfolding, a slow unseal,
a handshake with reality, a step in stride,
no place to rush, no need to hide...

The morning sunrays danced again
on a heart that knew both—joy and pain.
Birdsongs wove a new day's tale,
with acceptance blowing in the gale.

In the chambers of loss, I learned to see
life's balance—the bittersweet key,
to miss what was, yet cherish what's here,
to live and love despite the fear.

In the raw touch of grief,
acceptance found its grit,
a new texture, a profound knit.

And here I am—
my heart laid bare
with acceptance
woven into the air.

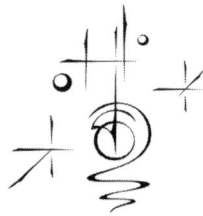

Acceptance
A Quiet Unfolding

Beneath the heavy cloak of silent tears,
I found my heart against a towering wall,
change, uninvited, barged in with no fears,
thrusting me into realities with no appeal.

Questions stormed the fortress of my mind;
Answers...
        oh, they were elusive to find;
Bargaining, denial, despair took their turns,
each leaving behind scars that burn.

In the moment between twilight's hum,
a light current of acceptance begun,
not with a shout or a roar,
but a quiet flow along the shore of my core.

It wasn't a battle suddenly won,
no triumphant end to a mournful run,
rather a subtle shift, a softening stance,
a tender surrender to the rhythm of the dance.

In the light of the moon,
in the warmth of the sun,
I began to see
the two could become one,
the sorrow that had cleaved my heart,
was making way for a new start...

Gently, the shadows began to lift,
and with it came an unexpected gift,
an understanding that in loss and gain,
joy and sorrow are but two sides of the same.

My heart still held remnants of what had been,
yet, in the silence, a melody unseen
played the notes of a song brand new,
sung with the words:
                              'It's okay, I accept you.'

I found the strength to hold both,
joy and pain,
to dance in the sun and walk in the rain;

With each new day acceptance grew,
a gentle friend, steady and true.

Acceptance,
it wove itself into the fabric of my being,
a quiet power, ever freeing;
Acceptance,
not as an end, but a beginning,
a thread in life's loom, endlessly weaving.

Life's painful brambles may ensnare us, yet within each tangled twist lies a hidden path.

By embracing the dance of resilience, we learn to tread the winding road with bare feet, feeling both the thorns and the earth's gentle embrace. In acceptance, we find the strength to discover joy amidst sorrow.

We walk not out of bravery but necessity, and in this walk, we uncover the pockets of happiness that live in the most unexpected corners of our hearts.

CAUGHT IN
A CURRENT

Between an inhale's hopeful birth,
and a sigh of exhale kissing Earth,
a universe unfolds, unspoken,
in the space between breaths broken.

I was given an ocean, stirring,
its depths unknown, its surface churning.
In diving deep, I came to know,
each wave was a tide of understanding returning.

A CURRENT OF MOMENTS

It's a heavy thing, isn't it, this cloak of grief? It weighs on the heart, drapes over the mind, and even the most familiar settings just don't look the same anymore. Everything feels distant, muted, like hearing a song but the volume's turned way down. There's this overwhelming sense of being out of sync, like you're tuned to a different frequency. And the big question I kept bumping into is "why?" A small word, but a profound one. "Why" tries to dig into the core of it all, tries to decode the enigma of life's changing tides. But "why," despite its good intentions, often leaves us stuck, doesn't it?

Instead, perhaps, we can softly, very softly, invite in a different question. Not with any force, not with any expectation of instant enlightenment, but with a quiet curiosity: "What's this for?" It's a gentle pivot that doesn't dismiss the pain or the struggle but nudges us into a fresh frame of mind.

"What's this for" doesn't promise to reveal grand universal plans. No, it's a more intimate, personal inquiry. It whispers, "In this place of pain, of change, of unpredictability, is there

something for me? Is there some form of understanding to be discovered, some strength to be gained, some deeper compassion for myself and others to be nurtured?"

It's like walking through a dense forest, this Life of ours. Sometimes, it's tranquil, and we can appreciate the beauty around us—the sunlight filtering through the leaves, the gentle rustle of wildlife. But sometimes, a storm rolls in, and we're lost, soaked, scared. And then, a single question, like a tiny beam of light, cuts through the turmoil: "What's this for?"

This light doesn't dispel the darkness. The storm still rages, the thunder still crashes. Yet the question can become a small but steady ray, guiding us through the murk. Not necessarily to a clear destination, but towards the next step, the next moment. And sometimes, that's all we can ask for—the strength to move through the Now, the courage to face the next Now, and the next...

In our living-breathing reality, each 'Now' melds seamlessly into the next, like the gentle, unending flow of a river, like the frames of a film creating a continuous, moving picture. The 'Now' we're in is not static—it's alive, dynamic, ever-changing. Every heartbeat, every breath, every thought we have is a unique brush stroke on the canvas of this continuous 'Now'.

When we find ourselves amidst the tempest of grief, it's easy to feel adrift, tossed about by waves of emotion, disoriented by the relentless winds of change. "What's this for" becomes a hand extended, not towards a far-off shore, but towards a deeper engagement with the present moment. It's an invitation to explore the depths beneath the surface turbulence, to recognize the richness and complexity within each frame of 'Now'.

And as we reach out, as we dive into the intimacy of the moment, we uncover new layers of understanding, new realms of empathy and resilience. "What's this for" encourages us to uncover the wisdom folded within our experiences, to recognize the potential for growth nestled within our pain, our confusion, our loss.

Each frame of 'Now' then becomes a space of exploration—a meeting point of what has been, what is, and what could be. It's a convergence of our past experiences, our present reality, and the potential paths that entwine into our future. When I ask, "What's this for," I'm not seeking to escape my current situation but choosing to fully inhabit it, to lean into its depth and breadth, its textures and colors.

The courage to face, to continuously enter the next frame of 'Now' is not about looking past my present or anticipating a future free of pain or struggle. Rather, it's about carrying the wisdom gained from each moment into the ongoing unfolding of my life. It's about the gentle yet transformative power of being fully present, fully engaged, fully alive within each frame of 'Now'.

And with each 'Now' we navigate, with each question we tenderly pose, we're woven deeper into the intricate fabric of life. We become not just observers but active participants in the grand, breathtaking dance of existence, remaining beautifully human in our shared experience of questioning, learning, growing, and simply being.

This silent conversation with ourselves is so personal and unique. There's no right or wrong way to do it, no map that fits all. But in those intimate moments when you ask, "What's this for?" know that it's not a solitary quest.

Many of us walk similar paths. Many of us struggle with our own storms, navigate through our own forests. And in sharing our experiences, our questions, our tiny beams of light, we find roots of silent understanding. We're all having our unique ways, yet, we are together in this grand, confusing, beautiful swirl of Life.

"What's this for" isn't a solution—it's a companion on the path, a conversation starter with ourselves and each other, a quiet song of resilience humming in the heart of our shared humanity.

What's this For?

Shrouded in grief, my heart clad heavy,
landscapes blur, life feels unsteady.
"Why?" I ask,
and glance back in vain,
but answers evade,
remain in yesterday's rain.

Then whispers a question,
gentle and bright,
"What's this for?"
it nudges, leaning into the light.

It doesn't seek grand plans,
or a treasure chest,
it asks, in this moment:
"What serves my quest?"

Life's like a forest, dense and wide,
in storms, I'm lost,
in fear, I hide.

Yet, "What's this for?" emerges,
a ray in the storm,
guiding me forward,
inviting transformation to form.

This silent dialogue within my core,
is unique and personal to explore.

"What's this for?" isn't a cure,
but a friend,
a song of resilience,
a guiding force,
a companion till the very end.

Transitions

On the edge of life's constant shifts,
where moments come and go so quick,
and deeper still each question drifts,
in solitude, my thoughts grow thick.

Yet, slowly, truth begins to click.

On a misty road, I walk,
                          foggy, unsure,
with thoughts clouded,
                          so heavy, so dense,
each step just led me to wonder more,
every pause made the silence intense.

"Why?" I cried to the silence with no pretense.

Deep in my sorrow, feeling my heart's heavy beat,
I caught a tune,
a never-ending song I wish I could repeat.

In the shouts, in the whispers,
in the silence that screams,
"Let it be," it sings gently,
pushing past my intense dreams.

Life's wild ride paints my story
in every sudden twist, in every gaping hole,
I etch my role, I find my place.

"There's no Why,"
the truth rings in time's space,
"Embrace the shift,
          let go of control,
                    let life set the pace."

In the silence,
when the world's buzz fades away,
a deep truth says its piece,
whispering that pain will someday cease.
Though the tears and heartbreaks
still seem fresh and frayed,
in shadows and light, Life continues its play.

In the craziness of living a whisper becomes loud,
chasing the reasons doesn't matter in the Now.
'But what's this all about?'
my heart wonders, showing me the way,
nudging me on into a tomorrow through today,
welcoming what may.

In our dance with life, so intimate and profound,
there's a heart-to-heart rhythm in every sound.
Each moment unfolds a beautifully human tale,
shared stories of us, through light, storm, and gale.

Amid life's constant turns and endless spins,
through laughter, tears, losses, and wins,
deep in my heart, one truth always shines on:

"Change is Life,
and Life is never done."

As the world continues spinning, it's okay to pause, to grieve, to look inwards, to heal at your own pace.

May you find comfort in the whispering stillness of time, reminding you that it is okay to move slowly, to breathe deeply, to simply be in the frame of now.

In the Frame of Now

In the frame of Now,
where life evolves,
a river of moments,
in which we revolve,
Each heartbeat's rhythm,
each breath we draw,
on the stretch of time,
each instance is real and raw.

My thoughts like the wind,
shaping the shifting sand,
my life but footprints,
left on time's strand.
Every emotion,
every dream,
every silent vow,
is a unique shade
in the frame of Now,
where joy dances,
and tears blend into the art,
here,
in the frame of Now.

Neither past nor future
can stake their claim,
only Now matters,
in life's vivid frame.

Every laughter, every sigh, every furrowed brow,
is captured and held in the frame of Now.

So breathe, live, love,
dare to thrive and to simply be
in the sacred Now,
where every heartbeat,
every thought,
every echo of doubt,
shapes this present,
leaves its trace,
in the frame of Now.

Through this moment,
through this breath,
we connect as one,
in the wonderful art,
in the frame of Now.

Between Breaths

In the quiet that settles between breaths drawn,
a silent world where Self is gone;
Here dwells truth stripped of the facade,
naked and pure, a silent pond.

Between an inhale's hopeful birth,
and a sigh of an exhale kissing Earth,
a universe unfolds, unspoken,
in the space where breaths are broken.

In the rhythm of this silent song,
where each beat to the next does belong,
the dance of existence gracefully weaves
a fine fabric of shared reprieves.

There, moments are not counted but felt,
in a timeless presence where Selves melt.
In the echo of silence,
boundless and wide,
truth lives, in which we all confide.

It's in this pause,
in quiet reprieve,
we have a chance to clearly perceive.
In the space that breath has left,
Life's deepest mysteries softly rest.

In the honesty of the unspoken,
in the peace of a breath broken,
we trace the outlines of our soul,
in the space between breaths,
we become one and whole.

In hearts that ache, where memories bloom,
a dance of Love through shadowed gloom;
A tender bridge between Now and Then,
a fleeting smile gives birth again
to whispered hopes, once sealed in frost,
in sacred space where nothing's lost;
A tiny flicker, brief yet bright,
illuminates an endless night.

BRIDGING ABSENCE

Today was a tough one. This morning, I woke up to a world that seemed indifferent to the heavy weight on my heart. The city was buzzing, the sun rose as always, and people's laughter filled the air. Life was carrying on as usual, but for me, it felt like everything was moving in slow motion, echoing the empty space inside my heart. All those once-familiar routines suddenly felt strangely foreign and out of sync.

In the midst of it all, the emotions were like a tangled ball of yarn, difficult to untangle and make sense of. Grief, heavy and profound, was like a fog casting shadows on everything else. Yet, even within this dense fog, there's an enduring glow —the glow of Love. The love that once was and still remains.

Today, this love reverberated through the strum of a distant guitar playing our song - the one we'd put on when the world felt too much, the one to which we'd dance ourselves silly. Just the two of us... a long time ago... in our tiny apartment. It was unexpected, yet it bridged the gap between the past and the present, offering me a gentle reminder that love endures and persists, even amidst my sorrow.

Every day brings new moments of connection to this enduring love. Some days, it might be an old joke remembered at the oddest moment, enough to bring a fleeting smile to my face, or a memory that kindles laughter through the tears. Other days, it's an understanding glance from a friend, a wordless conversation that vibrates in the quiet corners of shared sorrow.

The way through grief isn't linear, nor is it predictable. You might find unexpected moments of joy, of fond remembrance, intertwined with sadness. You know, these instances are not a betrayal of your grief, but a testament to the depth of your love. No matter how it surfaces, each of these moments serves as a tender reminder of the love that remains. And in their unexpected arrival, they provide me with small pockets of peace amid the complexities of grief.

Just like the ocean, our emotions are always in motion. They refuse to be boxed or contained, but instead surge and swirl, melding joy and sorrow into a poignant blend that reflects our inner world.

So, today, I found my heart mirroring the rhythms of the ocean, my emotions crashing like waves upon the shore. There were moments of retreat, where the heaviness of grief would pull back, only to rush forth again with renewed intensity, reminding me of the cyclical nature of our feelings. Yet within this chaotic flux, there was a strange kind of rhythm, a raw beauty in the honest expression of my heart.

As I move through the unknown, I'm learning to embrace the tumultuous tides. I cultivate resilience, tenderness, and a newfound appreciation for the beauty that lies in the nuances of my emotions. In this acceptance of life's unpredictable fluctuations, we find wisdom and healing. By gently releasing our instinct to guide every outcome, we make room for surprising moments, for new possibilities and spontaneity.

It's like stumbling upon a hidden gem in the midst of a bustling city – an unexpected surprise that could never have been planned or anticipated. Embracing uncertainty can be scary, but it also allows us to experience the richness and complexity of life in ways that are truly transformative.

I'm embracing the paradox, the chaos, and the beauty that exists within the elaborate and unpredictable performance of emotions. Each tear and smile, each moment of sorrow and joy, they are all part of me, signs of the profound love that will always remain.

May we find the courage to continue,
the resilience to heal,
and the grace to remember with love.

Through it all, I'm finding that grief and love are
two sides of the same coin - both a testament to the
depth and breadth of our capacity to feel, to connect,
to live.

Entwined

In the life's fleeting reprieve,
when sorrow weighs heavy on my chest,
I seek a haven amidst the tornado of grief,
in shattered worlds, I quest for rest.

Though darkness spreads its boundless wings,
a spark endures a flame that sings,
whispers of joy in hidden nooks,
where happiness blooms in life's small crooks.

Grief and joy, entwined they stroll,
hand in hand, through life's grand ball,
a dance of grace, fragile and fair,
revealing that solace resides in despair.

When sunlight breaks the clouded veil,
I'm learning that joy from within might prevail.
Even if fractured, my spirit mends,
on happiness' whispers my heart depends.

As I unravel life's terrane,
the highs and lows,
the grand and meek,
I find myself adrift, it seems,
in oceans vast of endless dreams.

Yet through the spectrum, I must feel
the joy and sadness, love and zeal;

for each emotion's shape, I quest
through the uncharted paths of life.

In heartache's grip,
the trivial gleams,
in friend's laughter,
and morning's sweet steam,
wrapped in blankets of warmth,
ordinary miracles,
that's where joy unfolds.

Within me lies the strength to strive,
to keep the light and hold on tight,
to cherish love and memories so clear,
and to let go lightly
of the dreams I nurtured dear...

In the Depths of Sorrow

When grief enfolds me in its mournful shroud,
the warmth of joy escapes my anguished grasp,
and in the depths of sorrow
I'm so tightly bound,
lost in a world that seems so far beyond.

Yet, even in the midst of pain and strife,
a tiny spark still flickers deep inside,
awaiting breath to kindle love's unclasp,
longing to break free from grief's grasp.

As I brave the night and seek that distant land,
where happiness and sorrow intertwine,
I'm learning how to hold grief's pain in hand,
and give my heart some time to heal and thrive.

Embracing aches and tears that freely flow,
the laughter born from memories once bright,
and in these moments,
healing seeds I sow,
and grant myself the gift of tender light.

Acceptance of my loss is not an easy go,
as I'm opening my heart
to embrace what life may ask.
In life's great pattern threads intertwine and flow,
the strength of human spirit weaves in kind.

From sorrow's depths, I'll rise again,
emerging with a Love that flows with warmth,
and though my heart may ache and bear the strain,
I find the strength to heal, while learning how to grow.

So, as I hold the pain and sorrow,
I find the strength to venture through,
because only in the midst of darkness,
I see the stars shine bright
and all their might comes true.

Craving Silence

In the heart of the carnival, yet alone I dance,
I wear a halo of laughter, but it's just a glance.
people flock around me, drawn to my radiant blaze,
in their eyes, I'm the sun, in a relentless daze.

In the core of the clamor, a ray I remain,
but my light feels like shadow, my joy is more like pain.
Drowning in the shallow, longing for the deep,
craving for the silence, where no words seep.

They gather for the laughter, the stories, the zest,
but who will sit beside me in the quiet of my nest?
Who will share the silence,
where no words need to impress,
where true connections belong,
within the sound of the unsaid?

My light may shine for others,
my soul – an open door,
yet within, lies a longing for much more.
More than just the surface,
more than the game,
in the silence and the depth,
a raw, wild, untamed flame.

In the space of chatter, an alien I stand,
longing for touch, not a hand.

In the bursts of laughter, my solitude hums,
in the speech of many, my silence comes.

So here I am,
the lively, the radiant, the bright,
Yet, in my world of many,
I seek a quiet night.
In the sea of conversation,
a solitary island I find,
in the heart of the crowd,
a lonely, beautiful mind.

It's in the depth of silence,
in the heart of the darkest night,
I am a lone star shining
in my own infinite right.

THE HEALING
I CAN HOLD

*Sometimes, it's not about thriving in the light,
but finding your light in the darkness.*

Beneath the dust of despair, joy stirs deep within,
a forgotten treasure, patiently waiting to begin.
Each spark of delight, each moment of peace,
are gentle reminders that sorrow will cease.

RESILIENCE IN MY FINGERTIPS

During those tough times, and even now, when the sorrow occasionally returns, I've sought solace in things that rekindle that warmth in my heart. You know, those favorite hobbies or cherished people who can make your heart flutter with happiness. I'm talking about my love for gardening, the feel of rich soil on my hands, the serene rhythm of planting and nurturing life, the joy of seeing a tiny seed grow into a blooming plant. It's about those quiet evenings when I lose myself in the world of writing, crafting narratives, and expressing my emotions through words.

And then there are the invigorating walks, my faithful dogs by my side, their tails wagging with every step. The simple act of reading, of diving into another world, getting lost and found in someone else's story. The therapeutic nature of drawing, the creativity flowing from my heart, through my hands, onto the canvas. And the joy of redecorating, transforming a space, making it my own.

Each of these activities required a different part of me. Some needed my nurturing spirit, others my creativity, and a few my physical energy. But they all shared one thing in common – they required my presence, my active participation in the moment.

These projects, be it decorating, crafting, or gardening, had another benefit. They allowed me to plan and look forward to something. In the midst of the turmoil, they provided a sense of purpose, a goal to work towards. They were islands of stability in the sea of uncertainty. And by spending time doing these things, I found myself reconnecting with the joy that was buried deep within. It was like brushing off the dust from an old, forgotten treasure, one which was there all along, waiting to be rediscovered.

Focusing on these positive moments, these sparks of joy, served as gentle reminders that there was still goodness in the world, even when I was going through the wringer. They reminded me that life, with all its ups and downs, still had the capacity to surprise, delight, and heal me. And that was an invaluable lesson.

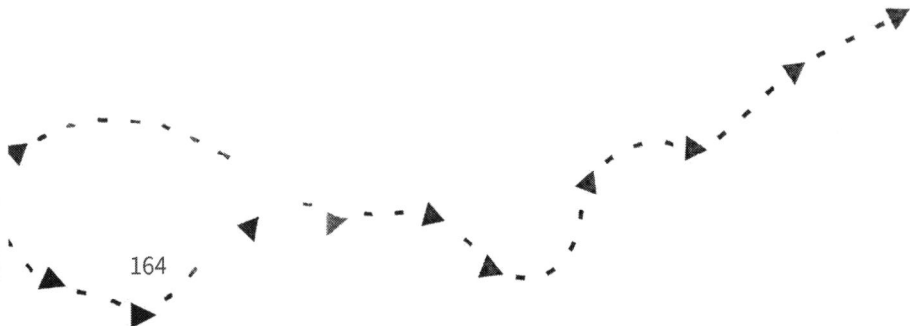

Directions

In gardens and writing, a comfort I find,
in companionship of dogs – a peace of mind.
Every seed sown, every tale spun,
a testament to moving on, with each rising sun.

In projects and passions, directions take hold,
in each stroke and line, stories unfold.
An anchor and compass in life's stormy sea,
reminding me gently of who I am and can be.

From the canvas of chaos, to a space of my own,
in each act of creation, my resilience has grown.

In every seed, every word, every artful line,
in silence and storm, in the everyday divine,
I seek
and I find
in the depth of despair,
a world without waiting,
a joy to declare.

The Sparks I Weave

Through seasons of sorrow, where shadows grow long,
I seek out solace where my heart finds its song.
In the whispering calm of a garden, under the soft sifting light,
with hands in the earth, my spirit takes flight.

Each seed is a promise, a secret unfurled,
in this richness of soil, I cradle the world.
From planting to blooming life hums its vibrant song,
In the rhythm of growth, my soul belongs.

When dusk softly settles, words whisper my name,
with a pen as my lantern, I kindle the flame.
Stories unravel, emotions set free,
swept by the currents of narratives I weave...

Strolling through twilight, dogs faithful and near,
in their wagging-tailed joy, all my troubles disappear.
A book in my grasp, I take flight through its pages,
lost and then found in other lives, other ages.

With a sketchpad and colors creativity flows,
from the heart through my fingers onto canvas, it goes.
In the joy of resculpting my space, each corner, each wall,
in the spaces I shape, I can see my all.

Each passion's a piece of a larger design,
calling for care, energy, a creative line.
But all demand my presence, active and true,

in these acts of creation I find my own view.

These projects, these passions, they light up the way,
give purpose and promise to each dawning day.
They're my anchor in chaos, my solace in the storm,
islands of calm in a world often torn.

Beneath the dust of despair, joy stirs deep within,
a forgotten treasure, patiently waiting to begin.
Each spark of delight, each moment of peace,
are gentle reminders that sorrow will cease.

Life's a spectrum, valleys and peaks,
but the capacity for joy forever speaks.
Through every struggle, every tear I've shed,
It's the art of living that moves me ahead.

Because in every stroke, in each seed, each line,
in the quiet and the chaos, the mundane and divine,
there's a song to be sung, a story to tell,
in the heart of creation, where I feel most aware.

A handful of soil, as simple as it can be,
yet within its grains a universe I see.
I touch it, feeling the cycle
connecting me to this place,
born from the earth,
to the earth
I trace...

FROM SOIL TO SOUL

There's a remarkable sanctuary, where traces of bygone days and the dreams of tomorrow dance within the heart of the earth. This isn't a mystical far-off place or a secret enclave hidden from the world, but an intimate corner, my very own backyard. In the quiet aftermath of loss, my heart finds solace here, basking in the gentle rhythm of nature, replacing the weight of sorrow with the soothing hum of life unfolding.

A handful of soil — it's as mundane as it gets, isn't it? And yet, within its crumbled richness, there exists a universe of life, teeming and pulsing. There's a truth to it, one that calls out to our primal selves. Touch it, let the grains fall through your fingers... I am a part of this grand cycle, born of earth, destined to return to it.

There's a healing quality to it, a soft surrendering. When I bend, it's as though I'm bowing down to the earth, and the earth responds by opening up, providing a comforting, nurturing feeling in return. The act of gardening is as gentle as a lullaby and as grounding as a mother's embrace. In that moment, I'm not just a gardener, but a child... a child of the earth, playing with the elements, tracing the rhythm of life.

I plant a seed, and with it, I let a part of my pain go. I'm giving it an opportunity to transform... transform into something vibrant and beautiful. A seed... It's a small thing, seemingly insignificant, a capsule of possibility in the palm of my hand... But it's more than just a seed. It's an act of faith, a quiet promise whispered to the winds. It's a testament to the endurance of life, a metaphor of resilience, embodying the journey from the depth of darkness to light.

The soil embraces my offering, a solemn pact between me and the world. The whispers of the earth — a rustle in the leaves, the cawing of a distant crow — they are the choir of life, a reassuring chorus that I'm not alone.

As the days roll by, the seedling within the soil begins its way cradled within the womb of the earth. It's not a flight from gloom, but a dance of life within a warm, comforting sanctuary. The soil is not a place of exile but a haven of nurturing safety, moist and alive, pulsing with the rhythm of existence.

Within this nurturing darkness, the seedling unravels, a testament to trust and transformation. It is here, in the heart of the earth, that the seedling understands the first stirrings of growth, the initial whispers of life. The darkness is not an adversary to be overcome, but an ally, a teacher, a tender cradle that holds and nurtures the seedling until it is strong enough to seek the light.

Roots reach deeper into the earth, tethering the plant to its nurturing source. They don't seek to escape; they seek to connect, to draw strength and sustenance, even as the seedling above stretches towards the sun. The roots and shoots, each moving in their direction, remind us that growth is not just a way upward but a balancing act between the depths, the width, and the heights, between the embrace of darkness and the call of the light.

Just as the seedling embraces both earth and sky, we too, find ourselves navigating the interplay of darkness and light within our lives. The earth, in its gentle wisdom, teaches me to find comfort in the darkness, to trust in its nurturing presence, just as we yearn for the brightness of the day. In the seedling's growth, I see mirrored my own resilience, my capacity to find balance, to grow through and with our darkness, reaching ever towards the light.

Embracing the darkness is not a retreat from life but an affirmation of it. It is an acknowledgment that even in the darkest of soils, in the heart of our grief and loss, life persists, and hope germinates. Just as the seed trusts the darkness to nurture its growth, we too can learn to trust in our ability to transform our pain, to bloom from our losses, to reach out

from our comforting darkness, towards the light of healing
and growth.

In the tender act of caring for another life, I inadvertently
find a pathway for my healing. As you nurture the seedling,
you find yourself being nurtured. Each leaf that unfurls, each
root that deepens, they are milestones in the process, markers
of your resilience, reminders of your capability to heal.

> And so, we continue.
> We water.
> We tend.
> We love.
> We lose.
> We grieve.
> We heal.
> We grow.

All of it, intertwined in a dance as old as time. The garden is
not just a place of growth, but a realm of recovery, a sanctuary
for bruised hearts and weary souls.

"Soil to Soul," isn't it? It's a gentle loop, a cycle of life that
holds us in its tender rhythm. In the simple act of gardening,
I find a poignant expression of my human experience — one
of pain, loss, resilience, and, ultimately – healing. Amid the
rows of seedlings, under the comforting shade of foliage,
within the whispering winds and the hum of the earth, I find
a mirror to my heart, a testament to my ability to endure, to
heal, and to grow.

Rhythmic Ties

In my backyard, a sanctuary lies,
in the place between yesterday's echoes
and where tomorrow's dreams rise,
in the heart of the earth,
under open skies,
my soul finds solace,
in its tender, rhythmic ties.

A handful of soil—a universe so grand,
teeming, pulsing, alive within my hand,
a truth calls out, primal and raw,
"I am the earth and the earth is my law."

Garden's lullaby is soothing, gentle,
a grounding embrace,
a moment sentimental,
a seed planted—a piece of pain released,
Life's grand cycle, beautifully pieced.

Between Earth and Sky

A seedling's journey, humble and small,
within the womb of the earth, it hears the call,
a dance of life, a testament to trust,
from the depth of comforting darkness, life is just.

Roots reach deep, shoots stretch high,
a delicate balance between earth and sky;
darkness is not an adversary, but a loving cradle,
a warm embrace, where life's stories are able.

Charting through life, through loss and gain,
finding comfort in darkness, amidst the pain,
in the gentle cradle of the night, we remain.

From Soil to Soul

In caring for another life I see a path,
a nurturing cycle, a gentle aftermath;
each leaf unfurled, each root that deepens,
a milestone in healing, as my heart sweetens.

Soil to Soul,
a rhythm tender and old...
In this dance of life our story unfolds.
The garden—a sanctuary for the weary soul,
a testament to endurance, making me whole.

Pain, love, loss, resilience...
a rhythmic flow,
amid seedlings,
under the comforting shade,
a mirror to our hearts, beautifully laid.

Bare feet on the soil—a sacred tangible link,
connecting my soul with the world's pulse,
my hands—gentle keepers of life's spark,
the rhythm of the earth pulsing in my heart.

I KNEEL BEFORE EARTH

I kneel before earth, my hands cradling the immense potential that slumbers within a single seed. Here, on this humble stage of soil and green, the ordinary act of gardening becomes an intimate dance with life itself, a profound form of meditation that gently guides me toward a deeper understanding of my place in this grand show of existence.

Barefoot, my toes curled in the cool soil, I feel a sacred connection unfolding, a thread that weaves me into the greater existence. The rhythm of the earth pulses through me, resonating in sync with my heartbeat. I am an active participant in a greater, beautiful, universal exchange: each inhalation a quiet thank you for the air gifted by the trees, each exhalation a humble offering to the plants reaching for the sky around me.

As I plunge my hands into the rich black soil, I sense the deep reservoir of life beneath me. It's as though I am gently tapping into a chronicle of existence that has been quietly inscribed by the countless organisms that have called this earth home. In this precious moment, I am feeling the profound interconnectedness of life.

Every seed that slips from my hand into the welcoming earth is an act of faith, trust, and hope. It is a soft-spoken dialogue between me and the earth, a promise of life to come, and an affirmation of life's tenacity. With each seed, I am not merely planting potential plants, but also cultivating resilience, nurturing hope, and sprouting dreams.

When I close my eyes and tune into the heartbeat of the garden, I can hear the earth's whispers carried on the wind and the harmonious melody of growth emanating from every bud. I feel intimately tethered to this vibrant, perpetually unfolding narrative of life, a testament to existence's incredible persistence.

In the heart of the garden, a serenity envelops me. Surrounded by the gentle rustle of leaves, the intermittent melody of birdsong, the rhythmic hum of life, my thoughts gradually quiet down. Worries lose their weight, and in the face of life's simple, undeniable continuity, my heart finds peace.

With every act of gardening, be it turning the soil or watering the plants inside my house, I am engaged in a silent mantra, a mindful repetition that roots me in the present and cultivates an inner garden of tranquillity. This is my meditation, my refuge. In tending the earth, I am also tending to myself, learning to weather life's storms and blossom in its sunlight.

Gardening, to me, is much more than a pastime. It is a tangible form of meditation, an intimate communion with life, a serene sanctuary where the simple act of sowing seeds becomes a means of cultivating inner peace. It is here, in the garden, where I am most grounded, most connected, and most alive. In the gentle rhythm of growth and the sacred sound of the soil, I find my meditation and my home.

Tending the Self

In the quiet refuge of the garden,
bathed in sunbeam's glow
and rain's gentle kiss,
I kneel,
hands cradling a seed,
a microcosm of life in a speck,
awed by the promise that patience will perfect.

Bare feet on the soil—a sacred tangible link,
connecting my soul with the world's pulse,
my hands—gentle keepers of life's spark,
the rhythm of the earth pulsing in my heart.

Digging into the soil,
cool, moist and deeply profound,
where ancient secrets quietly sleep,
with each breath, a shared exchange,
air, life, and love, in an endless range.

Cradling a seed,
I'm holding hope,
planting dreams,
learning to cope,
mastering the art of the tightrope,
a soft whisper to the patient earth,
a silent prayer of rebirth.

Eyes closed,
heart open wide,
sensing life on the rising tide,
welcoming the ride,
in stillness, hear the harmony
of wind, of life, of a growing tree.

Life flourishes in the soil's embrace,
unfolds in its gentle cradle
each seed's journey is a delicate race,
a tender fable,
a mirror of our shared existence,
a testament to life's persistence.

In the cradle of the earth,
I find peace,
my worries soften,
my thoughts cease...
I am a thread in the splendid weave,
in the garden's wisdom,
I truly perceive.

Every seed planted – a silent mantra,
every bud – a nascent sutra,
in the heart of the garden
I am free,
in a sanctuary where boundaries cease to be.

A Handful of Soil

A sanctuary within the earth's heart I found,
an intimate corner, a sacred ground,
in the quiet aftermath of my sorrow,
I learned how to dance
between yesterday and tomorrow.

A handful of soil, as mundane as it seems,
holds within its grasp life's intricate dreams.
I'm a part of this cycle, born of earth's flesh,
destined to return, yet ever refreshed.

To this nurturing earth, I bend and I bow,
a gardener, a child, an intimate friend,
in the act of planting, in the lullaby of leaves,
I fall into a healing rhythm, in which Love beats.

Each seed I plant—a pain I let go;
in the palm of my hand,
hope begins to grow,
more than a seed—a testament to life,
a spark of resilience bursting through strife.

From root to leaf to fruit that I bear,
each season unfolds with wisdom to share.
As the sun dips low, yet never depletes,
I find my soul's harvest in life's quiet beats.

Grounded growth is an intimate dance,
a meditation,
a chance for a silent romance.

A PROFOUND SENSE OF CONNECTION

Let's take a step beyond the poetry, the metaphor, and me, pouring out emotions. Let's talk about in a more tangible, dirt-under-your-fingernails kind of way, the experience of gardening. There is a rhythm to it, a steady beat that exists in the rustling of the leaves, the buzzing of the bees, the falling of the rain. But let's look deeper. You see, there's a form of meditation hidden within the folds of gardening. Let's call it Mindful Gardening Meditation, if you will.

Isn't it remarkable how the act of gardening invites you to be wholly present? There's something about the feel of the soil against your hands, the smell of fresh earth and plants, the sight of colorful flowers and lush green leaves. The gentle sound of leaves dancing with the wind. It's an immersive sensory experience that pulls you into the present moment, embodying the essence of mindfulness.

Gardening is our way of shaking hands with nature. I step into the garden, leaving the walls and screens behind, and become a part of the natural world. There's a calming, grounding effect in this. It wraps around you, gently encouraging a sense of peace and tranquility akin to the stillness we find in meditation.

Now, plants aren't fans of the rush, right? You can't speed-grow a flower or a tree. They move at their own pace, teaching us patience and appreciation for the slow unfolding of life. In a world that's often running at high-speed, gardening is a gentle reminder of the beauty in gradual growth.

Perhaps you've felt it—the quiet joy, the subtle lifting of spirits that comes with time spent in the garden. You know, this therapeutic effect, recognized and affirmed by numerous studies, resonates with the calm and clarity we often find in the quiet space of meditation.

In the garden, I cultivate more than just plants. I nurture care, patience, and persistence—qualities that resonate with the compassionate awareness fostered in meditation. Because, as you care for each plant, guiding it from seed to bloom, you practice understanding and patience. This cultivates a tangible empathy that reminds us of our interdependence with all living things.

This practice of care expands our capacity for compassion. Each moment spent in the garden helps us slow down, become more present, and opens our hearts to deeper feelings of compassion and connection. Just as the garden grows, so does our understanding and empathy towards all forms of life.

Though sitting quietly and breathing might seem worlds away from turning the soil and planting seeds, these two practices are rooted in the same values.

Both gardening and meditation offer pathways to mindfulness, tranquility, patience, and a profound sense of connection. The focus of that connection may differ—inward to the self in meditation, outward to the natural world in gardening—but both practices foster a beautiful, compassionate understanding of the intricate dance of Life.

And so, here we are, in the heart of a practice that fuses the soil with the soul. You've ventured through my words, feeling perhaps the stirrings of that deep, quiet place within you that resonates with the beauty of nature and the stillness of your own mind. But words are merely the first step on this path, a breadcrumb trail leading you deeper into heart of awareness.

If you're interested in taking this experience from the conceptual to the tangible, I've prepared some resources for you. It's a sequence of practices designed to root your attention firmly in the present, providing space for both internal and external growth.

Scan the QR code below and step into this expanded space at PositivePranic.com

positivepranic.com/garden

You'll find a series of Mindful Gardening Practices, designed not just as tasks but as rituals—moments in which you can deepen your connection to both the garden and yourself.

Grounded

In the cradle of nature, a sanctuary lies,
an open canvas under the sprawling skies;
Here, between soil and soul,
is where grounded growth quietly ties.

Each seed I sow, each root that takes hold,
is a mindful whisper, a story told,
of loss and of love, of growth and decay,
in the garden's embrace, I lose my way...

Breathe in,
breathe out,
kneel in the dirt,
planting my hopes,
healing the hurt,
with each caress of the gentle wind,
the boundaries blur,
the Self is thinned.

Look!
A sprout breaks free, reaching for the light,
a testament to resilience, bursting through the night,
in its silent growth, a mirror I see,
of my way, my growth, the essence of me.

With the rhythm of nature, my heart aligns,
in its comforting embrace, my spirit shines.

Grounded growth is an intimate dance,
a meditation,
a chance for a silent romance.
From the garden's heart, lessons unfold,
in each leaf, in each root, wisdom is told.

To be present,
to nurture,
to be,
in this dance with the soil,
I find me.

LESSONS FROM FURRY SAGES

The Wild Wisdom

You know, I was out in the backyard the other day, watching this squirrel. Its tiny claws gripped the bark with focused intensity. The world was alive in its black eyes, reflecting a reality... It was so focused on its task, rushing up and down the tree, busy with the day. And I thought, there's a little creature that just keeps on going, no matter what the world throws at it. It was oddly comforting while I was there, dealing with all this grief.

There's a peculiar paradox we humans grapple with. We stand rooted in our sorrow, our world seemingly stalled, while life around us pulses forward in an untamed rhythm. Isn't it strange how life keeps moving forward, even when you feel like you're stuck? It's a harsh reality when you're grieving. But then, when I look at the animals, I realize that they deal with loss too. And yet, they persist, they adapt, and keep on going. It's like they've figured out the balance of how to respect the pain but not let it stop them from living.

I once saw a documentary about elephants, about how they grieve for their lost loved ones. Elephants... those magnificent creatures steeped in wisdom and encased in a thick skin that belies their emotional depth. When an elephant loses a member of its herd, it mourns, standing vigil in heartrending silence. It struck me, you know. They take the time they need, they don't rush the process. It made me realize that it's okay not to be okay right away. Grief takes time, and we all move at our own pace.

And what about wolves? You know when they lose one of their own, they mourn, but they also lean on each other. They continue together. They remind me of the power of community, the silent solace of shared pain, the healing touch of empathy when solitude becomes a heavy shroud.

Then, I think about the butterfly a well known symbol of transformation, right? It's a silent testament to life's eternal cycle of change, of endings and beginnings. It's almost as if it's telling us that change, even when it's painful, is part of life. It doesn't downplay the hurt of loss but shows you can grow from it. It's okay to grieve, but it's also okay to let that grief change you, to make you see life from a different perspective.

And just as a butterfly emerges from its cocoon only after a period of inward reflection and transformation, we too often need periods of solitude and introspection. Change can be scary and often comes with a certain level of pain and discomfort, but these feelings are not only normal they are necessary.

It reminds me that patience is key during this process, to give ourselves the time to heal and adapt to our new realities. The butterfly doesn't rush its metamorphosis. It doesn't question the process. Instead, it patiently waits, knowing that each stage is necessary for its ultimate transformation.

You see, in a way, animals have taught me a lot. They show me how to be present, to experience my feelings, not to run away from them. They remind us that life, with all its ups and downs, in all its heartbreaking beauty, is in constant motion. Grief is a part of life. It's hard, it hurts, but it's also a sign of the love we have and hold dear.

So, when grief feels too heavy, I turn to nature. I find strength in its resilience, I learn patience from its rhythm, I feel less alone thinking about its sense of community, and I find hope in its capacity for renewal. We're all part of this big, messy cycle of life, and there's some comfort in knowing that we're in this together.

Treetop Tenant

In my backyard,
a squirrel and I cross paths,
two creatures—worlds apart,
each bearing life's wraths.
It clings to the tree,
a spark in its eyes,
short moments of stillness,
yet always on the rise.

It's busy, moving,
got places to be,
up and down, back and forth,
on that old tree.
And here I am,
sunk in my world of pain,
watching this tiny critter dancing in the rain.

Life happens all around, it doesn't stop,
up and down the bark, a tireless hop.
In its humble hustle, I start to see,
a mirror of us,
a mirror of me...

Here I stand, heart heavy with grief,
watching its scramble, finding relief.
Tiny but tough, it doesn't miss a beat,
against life's odds, it doesn't admit defeat.

Through rain or shine,
through loss or gain,
it carries on,
in joy or in pain.
Its determination,
its strength,
its quiet strife,
serves as a gentle reminder
of the rhythm of life.

Something stirs within me,
watching its strive,
in its tenacity,
I see my way to my will to thrive...

Tears of the Titan

From a trembling earth,
a titan falls,
not in battle, not in glory,
but in silence...
underneath Acacia's watchful sprawls,
no hero's end, no victor's story....

Another titan,
her shadow tall,
stands by the lifeless...
her heart aflame,
beneath the thick hide,
in her eyes wide,
pain
and an ocean of feelings,
she does not hide.

Rough skin on cold ivory,
a testament,
a goodbye,
a touch,
a fragment of the past...

Grief is not beautiful,
nor eloquent,
Just a ruthless void,
a blast...

She stands...
days become nights,
and nights turn to days;
each sunrise—a reminder of her alone,
each sunset—the spotlight on her disarray,
her heart—a graveyard of the love she had known.

In her silence, a scream resonates,
in the space between her and the fallen kin,
a universe of sorrow that never abates,
an abyss that swallows all that's been.

This is grief -
raw, unromantic, brutal,
not a poem,
not a graceful dance,
just an elephant,
by a body,
under the moon's pull,
wrapped in the shroud of a mournful trance.

In her mourning, the world finds a mirror,
reflecting the depths of a heart in despair.
Grief needs no translator, its language is clear,
a howling of loss that we all share.

Hear the song of the grieving elephant,
in her wailing—a mournful chant.
Her pain is so real, so poignant, so rampant,
etched into the rhythm of her heart.

From the trembling earth where a titan once stood,
in the pulsating silence of Acacia's hold,
a tale of a titan, her grief understood,
an intimate process of sorrow untold.

Her vigil, her pain,
under the moon's glimmering glow
a reflection to love's enduring flame,
in the face of loss, against the harsh blow,
bears witness of grief, of love, of life's claim.

Listen to the song of the grieving titan.
In her mourning, find your own heart's refrain,
her pain is your pain, a bond that loss can't sever,
in the rhythm of her heart, hear your own strain.

In her - see us, her grief is ours,
an intimate dance with the ghost of what was,
underneath the same indifferent stars,
a testament to the ties that loss draws.

She grieves...not for show, not for the skies,
but for the Love that death cannot smother.

A lesson to us:
when a part of us dies,
it's not just alright,
it's necessary to take time to recover.

...when a part of us dies,
it's not just alright,
it's necessary
to take time to recover...

Heartbeat of the Pack

Beneath the gaze of a moon unmasked,
in world wrapped in frost and shadows cast,
a lone song rises, slicing through the dark,
the raw, pained cry from the heart
of the grieving wolf pack.

They howl, they wail, their hearts lie bare,
every note a piece of the ache they wear.
In the silence, their losses laid out stark,
pain shared in the heart of the pack.

Yet from the ashes of their despair,
a truth as ceaseless as the winter's snow they declare:
their strength lies not in what they lack,
but in the relentless, united pulse of the pack.

No shield or armor in the biting air,
only the warmth of bodies gathered there.
In the face of loss, they do not turn back,
finding solace in the power of the pack.

We too stumble, falter, feel the taste of tear.
We too know the weight of loss
and the sting of fear.
Yet in each other, we may find the knack to live,
to love entwined as one united humankind.

Not in solitude, but in souls paired,
not in silence, but stories shared,
together, we walk life's rugged track,
bound by the love,
the pulse,
the heartbeat of our pack.

.

Self-Embrace

In the garden, a cocoon I find, waiting,
an unassuming mirror of my own state.
Alone, reflective, clinging to the branch,
an expression of solitude's strengthening stance.

Change stirs deeply, leaves us feeling adrift,
yet within the cocoon, there's a crucial shift.
Pain, fear, discomfort – they transform here,
a process I too embrace, year after year...

A butterfly, on the verge of flight,
transforms in darkness, hidden from sight.
In this seclusion, it silently weaves,
a tale of transformation that one perceives.

The caterpillar's cocoon, self-woven,
not as a punishment, but a quiet haven.
A place for solitude, for self-embrace,
for transformation to trace its pace.

Sometimes I too need that space,
to embrace my grief, to slow my pace.
Not a prison, not a plea,
but a moment to just be.

To feel the depth of my sorrow,
untethered from thoughts of tomorrow.

In the present, I navigate my way,
through the sorrow, through the gray.

In this moment, alone, it may seem,
I'm adrift in a somber dream.
But much like the caterpillar in its flight,
alone, in the dark, before the light.

I'm not alone in my cocoon,
in my grief, under my monsoon.
Here, in solitude, I discern,
to face my grief, not to spurn.

Like the butterfly, with its grace,
I find strength at my personal pace.

So, I breathe,
like the butterfly, patient and free,
through my grief,
as raw as it may be.
Yet, each moment, through our strife,
is but a beat in the rhythm of life.

Change doesn't have to be a storm's shout,
it can be a quiet awakening, a gentle sprout.
The butterfly reminds me, in its unhurried rise,
that growing at my own pace is not a demise...

Paws in Presence

I watched my dog the other day. You know the way he stands, his gaze affixed upon the dew-kissed grass or a leaf tumbling in the dance of the morning breeze? No tomorrow clouds his bright eyes, no yesterday shackles his little body. He is the zenith of being, a living mantra of the power of Now.

In his world, there is no hollow longing, no grasping for some elusive future. Every moment is total presence, where the divine ordinary unravels itself in the array of the senses. The sharp movement of a tail, the flick of an ear, a satisfied sigh... are all hymns of the eternal Now.

I can hear the silence in his stillness. It's not the absence of sound, but the fullness of being. He taught me a language that precedes words, a lexicon of the soul written in the silent dialect of living, breathing existence.

A dog's wagging tail, a cat's lazy stretch, are sentences in the discourse of joy that emerges when you make peace with the world exactly as it is. Life, unfiltered, unadulterated by the constant buzz of human thought, is poetry in motion. And our pets, they are its finest bards.

In times of heartache, when the world weighs heavy and our spirit wanes, they approach us not with empty platitudes or well-meaning advice. Instead, they offer us a safe harbor in the tempest, a warm, silent embrace that speaks volumes. They teach us that it's okay to simply be. To sit with your sorrow without seeking to change or escape it. To let your tears flow, knowing that even when the sky weeps, it's still regarded as beautiful. They sit by us, their gentle purring or steady breathing becoming a lullaby for our troubled hearts.

Our pets do not seek to fix us because they know that we are not broken. We are whole. They invite us to recognize our wholeness even in our suffering. In their silent, attentive presence, they remind me that beneath my human struggles, I'm a Life itself, capable of love, resilience, and infinite transformation.

Their way of being inspires me. What if we learn to stand in the gaze of the moon with the innocence of a kitten, or to lose ourselves in the ecstasy of a simple walk or a run, like a dog chasing a dragonfly? Are we, humans, capable of immersing ourselves so deeply in the present that we become the present?

Because in this moment, we're never alone. We're bound by the breath of life that animates the cat at our feet, the dog by our side, and the beating heart within our chests. And in this recognition, I find not only my shared communion with life but also the strength to navigate the uncertain seas of existence.

Our pets, our silent teachers, reminding us to hold each moment close, to cradle it with tenderness, because it is in these transient breaths of time that we truly live. To be as they are, completely and utterly here, is perhaps the most profound lesson they impart.

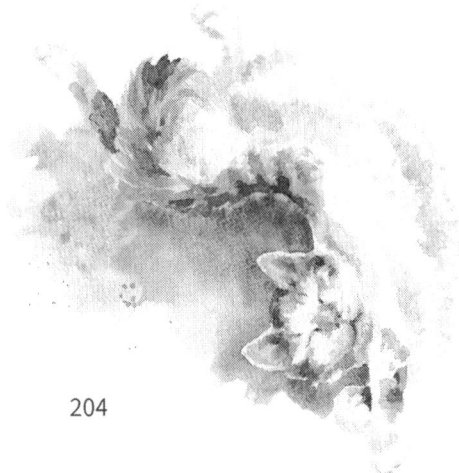

A Sage Without a Song

Each morning as I stir from dreams,
the first sight I meet is a pair of glossy eyes,
their tenderness so sweet...
patiently they watch, as night gives way to light,
and I open my eyes to love's pure delight.

My groggy grumbles met with the softest sigh,
hugs, snuggles, and kisses, are my morning's high.
His tiny soul, bubbling with zeal untold,
each sunrise, a new story to be unrolled.
With every ray, his excitement anew,
a fresh day, a unique joy to pursue.

For him, every dawn is a joyous parade,
as if seeing the morning sun for the first time,
unafraid his spirit soars, takes a joyful flight.
In his eyes, there's no mundane, all feels bright.

To him, each morning is a new birth,
a chance to spread his joy upon this earth.
He dwells in the moment's spree.
in his gaze, tomorrow doesn't play,
and yesterday has no sway.
In the raw freshness of the day,
he teaches me to embrace life's play.

He watches the leaf in a dance so free,
an embodiment of just 'to be'.
Unfettered by past or future's trace,
in the heartbeat of now he finds his place.

He does speak in silence, clear and pure,
life's deepest wisdom, he assures.
A dialogue deeper than words we convey,
in the quiet of the heart, it finds its way.

In his joy, in his peace,
I glimpse life's ceaseless lease.
A sage he is, without a song
singing of Now, where we belong.

When hardship looms,
he's by my side,
no hollow words,
in silence, we confide.
He sees no broken,
he sees no bent,
in his eyes, I'm whole,
no need for mend.

In his stillness, a lesson so clear,
in the ever-passing moment,
Life is Here.
My silent guide, he softly imparts,
to cradle each moment close to my heart.

His world,
a dance of the Present's song,
a reminder of where we all truly belong.
In his glittering eyes, the secret's key,
to Live,
       to Love,
              to Be.

Sweet Moment of Living

Sunrise kisses upon morning dew,
a baby's laughter, so sweet and true,
a soft breeze whispering through the trees,
the scent of flowers on a gentle breeze,

a steaming cup of fragrant tea,
an unexpected call from a lost good friend,
the crunch of leaves beneath my feet,
a favorite song that makes my heart beat,

a cozy blanket on a winter's night,
the sky painted with stars so ever bright,
a shared meal with those I hold dear,
the rustling pages of an old book I revere,

a long walk in nature's warm embrace,
the glow of the sunset's radiant grace,
the wagging tail of my sweet fluffy dog,
the calming rhythm of a crackling fireside log,

the scent of cinnamon apple pie,
a soothing aroma that lifts me high,
a genuine smile shared with grace,
a tender moment that lights up a face,

the warmth of sand between my toes,
the salty breath of ocean's whispers,
the way the gentle breeze caresses my skin,

as birds serenade with love songs
that make me glisten...

The simple joys that make my heart content,
as life's magic unfolds and beauty descends,
these moments are treasures,
too often dismissed,
all wrapped together as one precious gift.

This moment is all that I have
and all that is
for me to cherish
here and now,
as I embrace every heartbeat,
each laughter and tear,
because in this wonder,
true magic appears.

There's solace in movement, an understated language of revival that lies within us. Each stride, each breath, each stretch, is an unvoiced harmony, softly whispering of life that persists and joy quietly kindling beneath the surface.

Harmony in Motion

Walking alone among trees,
beneath a clear blue sky,
I paused to rest in the cool shade
where an enormous oak stood high.

Its roots dug deep, like buried thoughts,
anchoring it in the ground,
a quiet presence marking time,
in its silence, wisdom found.

Under the oak, away from the sun,
I felt a soothing calm,
a moment's peace in the gentle shade,
as if cradled in nature's palm.

The oak stood firm,
yet danced with the breeze,
as I watched its branches sway with grace,
teaching me a lesson of delicate balance
in the give and take of life,
in its rhythm,
in its steady pace.

Being strong, it seemed to say,
isn't about standing alone,
but flowing with life's winds,
to the unknown, fully grown.

The oak, in all its grandeur,
dancing in the daylight,
part of life's constant sway,
taught me to embrace the rhythm,
in its quiet, unassuming way.

Leaving the oak at sunset,
its silhouette against the sky,
I carried its silent wisdom,
its lessons, comforting as a lullaby.

Under the broad arms of the oak,
in the pulsing heart of the green,
I unearthed a part of myself,
in the quiet beauty of the scene.

Forest Whispers

Begin with a deep inhale,
full and clear,
allow the sensation of life to draw near.
Feel the air enter—a soothing tide,
let it wash through you,
with nowhere to hide.

See yourself as a tree, strong and tall,
reaching for the sky, yet embracing the fall.
Your roots, deep in the earth,
grounded and firm,
drawing life from below,
Life that nourishes and freely flows.

Close your eyes
and imagine the sun's warm light,
touching your skin,
making your soul gently ignite.
Each ray is a strand,
a story, a part of your weave,
interlacing moments
in the harmony you conceive.

In the silence of your mind,
let thoughts gently sway,
like leaves on a branch,
fluttering away.

Watch their dance,
as in the wind they tease,
acknowledge their presence,
then let them find ease.
allow them to be,
allow them to shift,
in this moment of quiet,
feel your consciousness lift...

Each breath you draw is a gift of life,
a moment of calm in the daily rush and rife.
Each exhale—letting go of the old and the worn,
creating space for peace, anew and reborn.

In the garden of your heart,
nurture compassion's seed,
a source of strength for you
and those in need.

Breathe in deeply,
feel the air fill your lungs,
you are a melody, in the universe, sung.
Each note—a vibration,
a ripple in time,
connecting you to the world,
a rhythm divine.

Each dawn brings a fresh day,
an opportunity to heal,
to love and to play.

As the sun dips down,
to the depth of the night,
embrace twinkling stars
as your guiding light.

Now, breathe out gently,
feel your body unwind,
leave behind all unwanted,
let peace of mind find,
in a radiant light,
you're a breathtaking sight.

See yourself as a tree,
still strong, still tall,
having embraced the sky,
and the fall after all.
Your roots, deeper now, in the earth,
nurtured by life's endless mirth.
Your branches swaying gently in the breeze,
each leaf is a whisper of life's ceaseless tease.

Each breath—a silent testament to life's grace,
You are Love in every trace...

Healing isn't a race against time. It's like gently unfolding a crumpled piece of paper. Our bodies and minds, wrinkled with experience, aren't broken puzzles awaiting completion; they're entire landscapes, as unique as we are. They carry not just the markings of our pain but also the silent promise of healing and happiness.

Each smooth stretch and deep breath unfolds at its own pace. These aren't steps towards becoming something new but rather acts of unveiling and rediscovering what has always been there. Because, as we move, we uncover fragments of ourselves that we thought were lost, along with the spark of happiness waiting to glow brightly once again.

MOVING THROUGH GRIEF

I found that moving my body, whether it was a slow walk in the park, a simple yoga sequence, or even just dancing around my living room like no one was watching, helped in releasing the tension knotting my body, and dissipating some of the heaviness. It was as though each movement was a wordless declaration: I'm still here, I'm still alive, and I'm finding my way back to joy.

And in those solitary moments of just being, of just breathing, I found more than comfort – I found glimmers of happiness that were still very much alive within me, patiently waiting for their time to shine again.

Accepting my pain wasn't about denying its existence or trying to escape from it. It was about recognition, embracing it as an intrinsic part of my life's pattern. My experiences—the happiness and sorrow, the losses and wins—all interlaced, creating a complex yet beautiful portrait of my existence.

So, I want you to know that it's okay to sit with your grief, to let the heavy feelings wash over you. But it's also okay, even necessary, to move, to stir the stagnant energy inside you. As I discovered, movement can be a great silent language of healing. It's like a conversation you're having with yourself, each stretch, each step, each breath whispering words of solace, understanding, and renewal to your soul.

But sometimes the world can seem too loud, too chaotic when we're grieving. We can feel lost and alone in a sea of noise and movement that feels unending, unyielding. Yet in those times, I remember that I have my body, my own world of senses that I can turn to, that can provide a different kind of solace.

You know, maybe it's the rhythm of your heartbeat as you walk, the comforting familiarity of your breath flowing in and out, the release in your muscles as you stretch – these are all testaments that despite everything, you're still here, still alive, and because of it, you are capable of feeling joy again.

I know, It might seem distant now, but it's there, somewhere within you, waiting for its moment to resurface. It's okay if all you can manage today is a tiny step or a single deep breath. Each one is a victory, a testament to your resilience, your inherent strength.

And as you move, there is no need to rush. Grief doesn't adhere to timelines, and healing can't be hurried. It's sort of like a dance that is unique to each of us. You might stumble, you might pause, you might take steps backward, and that's alright. Each day might not feel easier, but each day is a step forward, nonetheless. Your body will carry you through it, with more grace and strength than you may credit it for.

Your body is your ally in this. It holds the story of you, the laughter and tears, the love and pain. And while it carries the imprint of your sorrow, it also harbors the potential for healing and happiness. Just as your heart knows how to ache, it knows how to rejoice. And just as your body knows how to hold onto pain, it knows how to let go.

So, move, even when it feels tough. Do it gently, do it with kindness toward yourself. Let your body talk to you, listen to its whispers, its silent encouragements. Because within that movement, within that dialogue, you'll find pieces of yourself you thought were lost. Then little by little, step by step, breath by breath, you'll begin to see those glimmers of happiness grow brighter.

After all, you're not moving away from your grief, you're moving through it, toward a place where your pain and joy can coexist, creating the beautiful, intricate pattern that is your life.

Grief often makes us feel adrift in a sea of noise and chaos. But there's solace to be found in the simple intimacy of our own senses.

The steady rhythm of your heartbeat, the familiar dance of your breath, the release of a long-held stretch - they're the quiet affirmations of life that remind us: in spite of everything, we're still here, and joy is still within our reach.

I'm Here

On those heavy days,
when sadness clings,
when each moment stings
and hope barely sings,
I found a remedy,
subtle yet profound,
in the simple, healing act
of moving around.

Just a walk,
slow and steady,
under the sky's vault;
every step a subtle persistence,
every pause a halt.
"I'm here,"
my footsteps say, tracing the dew,
"I'm alive,"
they insist, pressing onto the new.

In my living room,
where only shadows cast a glance,
my body finds its rhythm,
it takes its chance.
In the spin, in the sway, in the dance,
"I'm here,"
my body whispers in its soothing trance.

The yoga mat—a canvas for my soul,
In every little bend,
in every simple stretch,
I play my role.
"I'm here,"
my breath assures me,
as I regain control,
"And I'll be here to weather any toll."

In quiet moments,
when the world's noise recedes,
not mere survival,
but something more my body breathes.
Through the ache, the pain,
still raw and sore,
glimmers of happiness
my body starts to explore.

"I'm here,"
my body softly speaking,
under the pain's hum,
quietly resilient,
it hasn't succumbed.
With each step, each breath,
as a new day greets the sun,
my body affirms,
"I am here, we've only just begun."

Step by Step

When the world is loud, and the chaos crowds,
it's alright to sit, to let grief admit.
Yet, within the still, stirs a hidden will,
a silent language of healing in moving and feeling.

The rhythm of my heart, as I pace,
my breath, a comforting grace,
the release in my limbs as they stretch,
whispers of solace in each etch.

Lost in the sea of noise and flurry,
alone,
in the incessant worry,
yet within me,
a different kind of peace,
my senses,
my solace,
my release.

The sound of my steps on the lane,
the flow of my breath, like soothing rain,
the release in my body, so profound,
proof of life in every sound.

It may seem distant, joy's soft glow,
yet within you, it waits to grow.
A tiny step, a single breath,
each a birth, each a death.

No need to rush,
there's no race to run,
grief dances at its own whim.
A stumble, a pause, steps gone astray...
each day a step forward, in its own way.

Your body is your ally, strong and brave,
holds your stories, every laugh, every rave
imprinted with sorrow, yet also with bliss,
it knows how to heal, it knows how to miss.

So, move, even when it's tough,
with kindness and love, gentle and rough,
let your body speak its whispers heed,
within its dialogue, you'll find the seed.

Lost pieces are found in the sway,
in the rhythm of life, in the play.
Step by step, breath by breath,
the glow of happiness, rebirth from death.

Remember when you last laughed until your sides hurt, or cried until you felt empty? It's your body that carried those feelings, and it's right there with you in every moment, sharing in all your experiences. It's more than a bystander - it's a partner. Maybe it's time we start treating it like one...

To My One and Only

My friend, my keeper, my love, all in one;
my precious body, my closest partner for life.
A body to cherish, a vessel to care,
it's not a short fling, but a lifelong love affair.

This partnership isn't so easy, it's true.
Sometimes I take two steps forward
and one step back, too...

Some days I'm just brutally selfish and pushy,
demanding respect for my frivolous will,
and blinded by notions that are seemingly grander and
smarter then the best adviser I have as my friend,
I foolishly ruled a self-demised game.

And during the times when I lost my way,
my body was seeing me through, day after day.
There were days when I was careless and even mean,
I took it for granted, like a spoiled little queen.

But my body never gave up on me, never once.
Through all the trials and tribulations
it kept me going without hesitation.
My faithful guide, my loyal friend in times of strife,
my closest partner for life.

My body knows me better than I know myself,
it whispers clues, when I'm feeling lost and unwell,
it warns me, when I'm pushing way too hard,
and urges me to rest, listen and be on guard.

It is my faithful guide and my loyal friend,
never judging, always there... till the very end.

It's seen me through heartbreaks and triumphs,
a steadfast guide,
helping me emerge stronger, with each stride.

Sometimes I forget to give my body the care it deserves,
but it never gives up on me, always ready to serve.
It reminds me to slow down, to breathe, to reset.
to take a break and recharge, to give myself rest.

In this lifelong love affair, I'm the first to admit,
my body is a much better partner, never throwing a fit.

I owe it not just my love, but my life too,
for carrying me through thick and thin,
lifting me up to begin anew.

In this relationship, there will be highs and lows,
but the most important thing is to be present
and to show
Love, respect and support, attention and care,
and together, we'll be a team through all we'll share.

JULIA DELANEY

228

FROM
SHATTERED
TO
SHELTERED

Like a bloom beneath winter's shroud,
frostbitten,
> *quiet,*
>> *unbowed,*
thawing slowly beneath spring's embrace,
healing happens at its own pace...

THE KINDNESS YOU KEEP

One thing I learned is that kindness towards oneself is crucial. Self-kindness is another very challenging aspect of my way through grief and loss. It might be tough because I often judge myself more harshly than I would others. I tend to set high expectations for myself, and when life becomes challenging, I tend to blame myself for not being strong enough, not moving on quickly enough, or for the circumstances that led to the loss.

I realize, I often subject myself to a sort of scrutiny, a harshness that I'd seldom inflict upon others. It is almost as if I have a reservoir of kindness within me. I willingly and happily tap into it when it comes to others, but when my own reflection stares back from the still surface, I hesitate. Instead, I fortify myself with tough armor, expecting resilience in the face of despair, chastising myself for not being impervious to the shrapnel of shattered dreams.

It's almost as if you expect yourself to be the mighty oak standing unyielding in the face of a storm. But even the strongest trees sway in the winds, surrendering to the rhythm of nature, and therein lies their true strength. The expectation to stand tall, to not be swayed by the winds of grief, can be an unbearable weight. And the blame we cast on ourselves for the circumstances that led to the loss—that's a jagged pill, indeed.

You see, the underbelly of grief is more than just the loss itself. It is the avalanche of self-blame, the gnawing guilt, the relentless questions: "Could I have done more?", "Could I have been more?" These inner demons twist the dagger of loss, adding an extra layer of suffering to our sorrow.

In this labyrinth of loss, I've discovered that self-kindness is not just a choice, but a necessity, an essential lifeline. It's that soothing balm for your raw and tender heart, that comforting blanket against the frosty winds of guilt and blame. It's about recognizing the whispers of your own pain, giving yourself the same understanding and compassion that you would bestow upon a cherished friend.

I think of it like being lost in a snowstorm—there's a tendency to fight against the blizzard, to push through the icy gusts with sheer force of will. But perhaps the real courage lies in hunkering down, in making a shelter, in being kind to yourself until the storm passes. Maybe, just maybe, it's about tending to your own wounds with the gentle touch of self-love, allowing yourself to heal at your own pace, like a frostbitten bloom slowly thawing under the warm touch of spring.

Sometimes, you need to be your own hero. Sometimes, you need to extend your hand to your sinking self, offering a lifeline. But being a hero doesn't mean being unbreakable. It means acknowledging your breaks, your pain, and cradling your own wounded heart with tenderness. It means giving yourself permission to feel, to hurt, to heal.

Self-kindness. It's about saying to yourself, "It's okay, you're doing your best. It's okay to not have it all figured out." It's about understanding that it's alright to stumble, to fall, to not know the way. It's about shedding the armor of false resilience and embracing the power of vulnerability.

And in these moments when my inner critic rises again, I remind myself that I'm not alone in this struggle. Many others go through similar experiences, just like me. We're all deserving of compassion, love, and support. I've found it's easier to remember this when I think about how I'd treat a dear friend going through the same thing. After all, we all deserve the same kindness we readily give to others, don't we?

So, on this road, I've been learning to extend the same compassion to myself that I'd offer a close friend in the same situation, I'm learning how to cradle my pain with the same tenderness that I would extend to a dear friend. It's about realizing that the gentle touch of self-kindness—that whisper of self-love—is a key part of navigating our way through the labyrinth of loss. In the delicate dance of healing, the tender steps of self-kindness are the rhythm of your resilience.

Heal Your Heart

positivepranic.com/LovingKindness

This guided meditation helps us to be more compassionate to ourselves and others. It counters the feeling of loneliness and a sense of separation. We can learn to be gentler with ourselves and quiet the internal monologue of self-judgment.

The Frostbitten Bloom

In winter's chill, a lonely flower stands,
its petals kissed by ice, not loving hands.
It trembles under a moon so cold and bright,
alone in a frozen world, a single point of life.

The snowstorm screams,
"Give up! You'll never win!"
But a quiet voice inside says,
"The battle is within."
It finds it doesn't have to fight the storm,
just nurture its own warmth,
its own inner norm.

No more fighting gusts that can't be tamed,
it focuses inward, and feels less ashamed.
It lets go of judgments, like falling snow,
and finds in its core, a gentle, warming glow.

Does it doubt, as the frost seals it away?
Maybe, but it also knows it'll see a brighter day.
It thinks to itself under the night sky,
facing its struggles, not questioning why.

That inner voice, once so quick to tear apart,
is stilled by love, by an awakening heart.
A lesson emerges, simple and true,
Kindness starts within, it starts with you.

Even encased in ice, it remains free,
warmed by a love only it can see,
unlabeled,
        unhindered,
                untouched.

When my dreams crack and tear me apart,
I think of the flower, how it found a fresh start.
I let kindness in, not as a show,
but as a first step, like a tender flower under snow.

It's not the frost that defines us,
but the warmth we maintain despite it.

The Shower of Life

A gentle rain,
an embrace so warm,
it soothes the soul,
wipes away the pain,
eases the storm.
Yet, at times cold,
like icy blades,
it strikes with a force,
no chance to evade.

With pressure strong,
it rasps and scrubs
the hardened crust with an icy blast.
Scouring away the past,
it opens the eyes
to a world so raw,
so simple,
yet wise.

It reveals an eternal bond
connecting all,
within reach and beyond.

Now my vision is clear,
and I timidly gaze,
at a shower of life,
as its beauty unfolds.
Feeling exposed,
open-hearted, yet bold,
I embrace all that life has to behold.

I see what's essential,
what to retain,
Now,
refined through pain,
I feel new again,
after the rain...

I see clearly now,
the world that's unveiled,
its raw beauty unassailed.

The things I need
are always here,
awaiting my reach,
here,
where they've always been,
and always will be...

Tender

Tender as a bloom claimed by the frost,
Its vibrance, for a time, seems lost.
Patiently it bides beneath the snow,
waiting for spring's warmth to help it grow.

Sometimes, the hero we require,
is not the one who conquers fire.
But rather, the one who understands,
the healing power of their own hands.

Being invincible is not the goal,
it's more about healing the soul,
acknowledging the scars we bear,
cradling our wounds with utmost care.

Grant yourself the liberty
to grieve,
to falter,
to question,
to believe.

Like the frostbitten bloom, we too awaken,
underneath the warming spring skies.
In the face of hurt, of fears untold,
I learned that tender Love
cradles courage in its gentle folds.

Where Self and Silence Meet

In places unseen,
where inner fights are fought,
there's an oak with all its might,
trapped by expectations,
caged by its own thoughts.
Its power isn't in rigidity or clenching tight,
but in the letting go and yielding,
accepting the storm's chaotic flight.

The giant, though in quiet dignity it stands,
must dance with gusts
that Nature's hand commands.
Its roots entrenched,
yet in the sky it sways,
true strength is found in rhythmic disarray.

The weight we carry is a self-set stake,
a heavy burden, like an oak in rigid state.
Beneath the strain of guilt and haunting fear,
the heart, in humble surrender, finally bends,
and in that yielding, the struggle ends.

In cavernous depths of grief,
self-blame finds no relief.
It gnaws and eats away, a relentless beast,
feeding on joy's marrow, in unending feast.

Could I have loved more, stood stronger in the fray?
Ghostly questions rattle my peace,
they sting like an old wound, refusing release;
a lament echoing through the chambers of my heart,
like a lonely bird's cry in the encroaching dark.

I'm embracing this truth, while my soul in torment tossed:
in yielding, not defying, no battle's lost.
Like the oak that dances, graced by tempest's hail,
in life's winding river, we must learn to set sail.

I embrace the tempest, the guilt, the mournful night
as woven threads in life's intricate fabric,
intimate and light, yet holding us tight.
In its grand unfolding, it's clear to me:
true strength emerges from fluidity.

From deep within, where Self in silence flow,
a sapling rises, its tale yet to grow.
Embracing storm and calm, guilt and glee,
it learns to dance in acceptance.
Now it's free.

IN SEARCH OF KINDNESS WITHIN

Here I am, just another person living, breathing, and feeling, much like you. There are days when life feels a little too heavy, a bit too messy. Days when it seems like the world around me is in fast forward and I'm stuck in pause. Caught in the aftershock of a shattered self, I would sometimes become lost within my own reflection. Amidst all the fragments, I would try to figure out where the pieces should go—or if they even fit anymore. And it hurts... it does...

Oftentimes, the world outside seems pretty chaotic, right? Everyone hustling, bustling, darting around, like they've got it all figured out... And then there's the world inside us—it's like a reflective mirror. A personal echo chamber filled with all our hopes, fears, dreams, memories, expectations.

Often, we become our own harshest critics within that echo chamber... I know I do... I whisper sharp words and they bounce back at me louder, harsher. The interesting thing is that I understand very well that those whispers aren't the whole story. They're just fragments of it, no more defining of me than a single pixel of a vast, vibrant portrait. Yet, I still do it... I turn my flaws into canyons, my mistakes into mountains, painting a landscape of judgment and expectation.

You know, when I comfort a friend, I don't just see a single pixel. I try to see the full picture. All the colors, shades, shapes, and outlines that make them who they are. I tell them it's okay, that they're human, that they're more than their pain, their flaws, their mistakes. And I mean every word of it.

I listen to them, to the harmony of their being, in all its complexity, its highs and lows, its crescendos and diminuendos. I extend my hand in compassion, my heart in understanding. So why then do I reduce myself to a single, discolored pixel? It doesn't seem to be fair, and it's not true...

For all my awareness, all my understanding of self-compassion, it can feel like trying to catch the wind sometimes. I see it moving the leaves, I feel it against my skin, but when I reach out... it slips through my fingers. It's there, it's real, but it's not tangible, not holdable. And it's frustrating because I know it's crucial, I know it's necessary.

I have no problem offering kindness to others, wrapping them in words of comfort and understanding. Yet, when it comes to myself, it's like I've hit a wall. I stand before it, armed with all the right tools, but still, I hesitate. My hand quivers, the words waver.

Why is it so difficult to extend to myself the same kindness I offer so freely to others? Is it because I fear complacency? Or am I just so used to the hard shell I've built around myself that any attempt to soften feels like an insult? It's a strange, paradoxical dance, this journey of self-compassion. I know the steps, but my feet falter...

But what I'm coming to understand is that not every change is an ordeal, though this one certainly feels like it. The path of self-compassion has its own unique set of challenges, tailor-made to trip me up. But it's a path I need to walk, no matter how many stones are in my way. So here I am, standing before that wall, or maybe even a mountain, willing to start chipping away. Not with a hardened jaw, but with a deep breath, patience, and the quiet resolve that this, too, can be navigated—one careful step after another.

At the end of the day, being kind to yourself doesn't mean you're settling. It doesn't mean you're giving up. It means you're giving yourself space to breathe, to heal, to grow. It means acknowledging your humanity, your right to falter, to feel, to be. And that's not just okay, it's necessary.

So yes, the journey of self-compassion for me is not a walk in the park. But I am committed to keep trying, gently... to keep learning. Because I know that every step, every stumble, every fall, it's all part of the process. And it's a process worth undertaking, for myself, for my growth, for my peace. After all, we're all deserving of our own kindness, aren't we?

The Last to Cast

In the still of night, in day's harsh light,
a quest stirs within, challenging, yet feels right.
Echoes of judgment in my mind's expanse,
yet kindness to others I freely advance.

We're more than mistakes, more than pain,
an art piece, not a single astray stain.
Why then do we offer empathy so vast,
but when it comes to self, cast it last?

A humble seed can birth a forest grand,
a hidden strength that can expand.
So too can self-compassion be,
a quiet power, setting us free.

Why does the self-love dance seem tough?
The rhythm known, yet not enough.
It's not giving in, it's taking the stride,
on the way to self, an essential ride.

Again and again, I trip on life's stage,
stumbles and falls are part of the play
in life's grand theater—The Everyday.

But each fall reveals a truth untold:
by embracing the rhythm, accepting the sway,
through self-compassion, I'm finding my way.

Beyond the Echo Chamber

Here I stand, on the edge of thought,
where the Universe's vastness is caught,
in the echo chamber of a single mind.
Where does the line between us unwind?

Is it in the heartbeats that time our tale,
or the silent spaces where words fail?
In the dance of life's grand array,
where does self-kindness find its way?

If a soft word can warm a heart,
can self-kindness be a gentle start,
to healing wounds and scars unseen,
in the echo chamber where we've been?

We learn to nurture, to extend our grace,
to every living, breathing space.
But do we know how to retreat,
into our quiet, hidden inner street?

Can we be kind when no one's looking,
when there's no one else's approval hooking,
onto our actions, our spoken words,
can kindness still be what our heart asserts?

Is self-love silent, does it shout,
or is it a whisper when we're worn out?

247

In the depths of night, in the break of day,
is self-compassion the first to stay?

In the language of the stars, does it speak
a love that's resilient yet knows how to heal?
In the heart's beat, in the mind's play,
is self-compassion leading the way?

From the spark of youth's bright fire,
to the wisdom that the years acquire,
does self-compassion leave a trace,
a gentle imprint, a saving grace?

The personal path winds, but we're never alone,
in our hearts, seeds of kindness are sown.
Each misstep, each rise and fall,
is a step on the journey, through it all.

So here I stand,
on thought's precipice,
where Love's voice rings clear in a single mind's abyss,
where the line of Self and Other ceases to persist,
in this echo chamber, where our thoughts coexist,
in the lines etched on the palm of my hand
there's a kindness that quietly persists,
in my existence, it insists.

In Plain Sighs

Beneath my nose, a secret lies,
wisdom so profound, hidden in plain sight.
In each inhale, each gentle sigh,
an endless rhythm beneath the inked sky.

A gift so simple, so mundane,
yet, it's power is anything but plain.
In every moment, in every scene,
breath takes the lead, yet hardly seen.

My constant companion, day and night,
dismissed, unseen, unfelt, yet holds me tight.

Its rhythm humming a simple song,
in its simplicity, I belong.
A wisdom there,
right under my snout,
it's always there, without a doubt.

Yet it's a treasure I have to 'earn',
in each breath, life's secrets I learn.

So, I inhale...
exhale...
and let it be..
In this dance,
I'm free.

The wisdom of breath,
so close, so near,
in its silence,
life becomes crystal clear.

So, I celebrate this universal joke,
in each breath I let my heart soak.

In this rhythm let's immerse,
Life's wisdom is in each breath's surge,
a truth so clear, yet often overlooked,
found right beneath our very nose,
in each inhale, a shared compassion grows.

The Magic of Cyclic Sighing:
The simplest way to reduce
stress and make you feel better.

positivepranic.com/sigh

NAVIGATING THE SILENCE

Whenever I felt the weight of the world heavy on my shoulders, pressing me down into an unfathomable depth, I discovered solace in the simplest of acts: just breathing. Taking those moments to pause, to truly feel the breath coming in and out, the rhythmic rise and fall of my chest...these became my anchor points, bringing me back into the present.

I introduced a regular practice of meditation into my daily routine. Each deep, intentional breath seems to blow on that tiny flicker of happiness still living within me, causing it to glow just a little brighter each day. I'm well aware that meditation doesn't come naturally to some. But with patience and consistency, many people find a deep calm within, just like me.

So, for the seekers of inner peace: just like a novice painter or an untrained musician, it starts with understanding the instrument at hand. Our breath is this instrument—seemingly simple, yet astoundingly profound. When you pay close attention, the rhythm of breath becomes a silent symphony, resonating with the pulse of life itself. Each inhale brings a wave of fresh energy, rejuvenating the soul, washing over our internal landscape. Each exhale is a release, an opportunity to let go of tension, to dispel clouds of anxiety, to surrender the heaviness that burdens us.

It's in these pauses, these spaces between breaths, that the magic of meditation unfolds. Here, we come face to face with our most authentic selves, unadorned by the trappings of external validation or societal expectations. Here, we find silence; and in that silence, we unearth our inner wisdom.

In this quiet sanctuary of breath, I find a solace that's not a mere escape, but a homecoming. I return to our essential nature, untroubled, unhurried, and unfettered. And it's in this return that the spark of happiness grows brighter, warmer, turning into a comforting flame that illuminates our inner world.

By tending to this flame through regular practice, we cultivate resilience. We learn to weather storms with grace, to dance with uncertainty, and to embrace the beautiful impermanence of life. This way into the self, guided by the rhythm of my breath, reminds me that tranquility is not a distant goal, but a state of being accessible in the Here and Now.

Meditation doesn't promise an escape from life's challenges. Instead, it offers a lens to view them with clarity and courage. It equips us with the strength to navigate life's maze, turning stumbling blocks into stepping stones, and hurdles into opportunities for growth.

Breathing Life

In the quiet cradle of each breath,
life and death are interwoven in depth;
an eternal cycle, so grand,
that whispers tales of countless sand;
an intimate exchange, yet vast and deep,
that unfolds in the silence where I steep.

Breathe,
exist in the Now,
in the seen and unseen's vow.
In each breath, truths unmask,
every breath
is a dance with life,
a dance with death.

Each inhale—a new beginning,
each exhale—a cycle spinning.
In this dance, life gains its pace,
with each breath, time we trace.

In every breath, a key to being,
I embrace,
a world within, constantly in grace.
The rise and fall,
the gentle sway,
with each breath, I'm in the play.

While breathing life, I meet my soul,
in this rhythm, I am whole.
Each breath a whisper, a secret told,
in the heart of life, I take hold.

So, I breathe in, the world in flight,
and with each exhale, I shed the night.
In this dance, there's just the 'Now',
in breath's rhythm,
Life's essence I allow.

Boundless Ties

Just as a baby through the cord to the mother is tied,
we're bound to existence through breath, our guide,
an anchor within, to which we can always return,
in the rhythm of life this wisdom we earn.

In the absolute stillness, beyond exhale's end,
Life's wounds, in silence begin to mend.
A moment of quiet, a pause in the tide,
capturing the rhythm of life,
beneath the skin... deep inside.

Each pause is an unspoken verse,
an infinite space in the blink of a sigh.
In the silence between the rise and fall,
lies the secret that unifies.

Beyond the clamor of thoughts that stray,
in the stillness, truth finds its way.
A whisper of peace, a sigh of release,
in the silence, I find my ease.

In this space I am free,
unbound by time in unity.
Each pause, a gateway vast,
anchoring me in the present,
where time abundantly lasts.

In my breath, I found a life that outlasts death.
The rise and fall is a silent song,
in its rhythm, I belong.
Each breath, a bridge between you and me,
a connection deeper than language can be.

Just as a baby, bound by the cord,
finds its existence in a mother's word,
we, too, are tied to the vast universe,
through breath, our eternal verse.

In the rhythm of breath,
so subtle, so sweet,
in the grandeur of life,
like mother and child, we all meet.

In this dance, we are one,
in the cycle of the stars, the moon, the sun,
in the pause, in the quiet hum,
I discover that I am,
we are,
all is one.

Healing Ripples

Breathe in gently, deeply now,
your body's wisdom showing how,
let your chest rise and fall,
in this moment, allow
your heart to hear its own call.

Close your eyes,
see the night,
the stars glittering above,
shining brightly from afar,
each one a memory,
guiding you no matter where you are.

In the softness of the stillness,
after each breath's end,
a silent haven where healing is kept.
A moment of quiet,
a pause in the dance,
feel the rhythm of life,
let your heart reset.

Breathe out slowly, releasing the hurt,
allow it to float away, lost in the dirt..
Like leaves caught in a gentle wind,
moving towards a place where spring begins.

In the canvas of your mind,
sketch a world that's kind,

where love and peace are intertwined,
let go of what's left behind,
with each breath
nurturing your inner light.

Every breath you take
creates soft, gentle waves in a healing lake,
each pause offering your heart a break,
each exhale is a ripple you make,
in the stillness,
feel your heartache,
let the weight recede,
with exhale, let your pain be freed.

Breathe in serenity,
breathe out discomfort...
like a summer's gentle rain,
washing clean life's window pane,
revealing a clear sight
free of storm clouds' shadows,
free of winter's frostbite.

Each inhale, a new beginning,
each exhale, a gentle unspinning,
in this dance, this eternal spinning,
you are growing, you are healing,

Feel the love that surrounds you,
the universe's energy flows through,
each breath is a reaffirmation ringing true,

you are cherished
you are here,
you are loved,
you are whole.

Breathe in gently, deeply now,
your body's wisdom showing how,
as your chest rises and falls,
let the rhythm soothe your soul
and at this moment, allow
your heart to hear its own chant,
You are Love,
embrace it all,
let it console.

On this path, you're not alone,
connected by unseen threads,
you're intimately known.
Across the universe,
these connections have grown,
linking us all in a healing tone.

Breathe out slowly,
feel the release,
each breath bringing a sense of ease,
in this moment, let all worries cease,
You are Love,
You are Peace.

JULIA DELANEY

GRIEF'S
DECEPTION

Because we love—we grieve, it's life's refrain;
Without Love, Grief's essence we can't explain.
The more we love, the more we bleed and heal,
but in the heart of it all, there's a truth we feel.

THE UNENDING BREATH OF LOVE

Grief has this one sneaky way of settling in. You know, that quiet whisper that winds its way into your thoughts, a whisper that slinks around in your mind, hinting that if you stop feeling this pain, if you let go of your grief, you're letting go of the person who isn't here with you anymore. It's almost as if you believe that to stop mourning is equal to forgetting and that forgetting implies the love is lost or wasn't real...

It's a little like trying to hold onto wisps of a dream, a dream that was once so alive and real. You're standing amidst the afterglow of an illusion, picking up the pieces of a life you thought was eternal. This grief, this vacuum they've left behind, can feel like the only thing you've got to remember them by, the last vestige of a love you're scared might vanish if not for the ache it leaves.

But here's something you may not see right away. As the raw wound of grief begins to heal, a quiet transformation takes place. The turmoil of loss eases into a stillness that reveals a new understanding of Love. Your love doesn't get boxed in by hellos or goodbyes, it doesn't end with life or death. It's something of its own, untouched by the chaos and change of life.

Grief might be a heavy coat you're wearing now, but Love, Love is a force of its own. Love doesn't get left behind in time or space or the physical world. It endures, a shining light that outlasts everything else. Embracing this brought a breath of warmth to the cold of grief; a gentle nudge that even in my sharpest pain, the warmth of love I shared is still here—bright and unchanging, a testament to what once was and what still is.

We grieve because we love. This isn't a concept, not an abstract thought. It's an experience, a reality that grips us, roots us in place, and makes us painfully aware of our own hearts and their capacity to feel.

In moments of quiet, I often find myself reaching out to trace the edges of a grief that is ever-present. It's in the most mundane of things: a melody hanging in the air, an unfinished conversation, a shared joke now lingering in a silent room. Our hearts remember... and in remembering, ache with a love that extends beyond the realms of physical presence.

There's no standard way to grieve, no roadmap that can lead us out of the maze of loss. It's an unchartered journey that we navigate differently. Grief can be loud, filled with cries and shouts, an attempt to reach out to a loved one who is no longer within grasp; It's a silent scream, a whisper lost in the wind, a solitary tear tracing its path down a cheek.

The deeper we love, the greater the tide of grief that washes over us. It can be terrifying—feeling so much, bearing so much. It's as if our hearts, once filled with shared dreams and whispered promises, are now vast landscapes of longing and remembrance.

Yet, isn't it profoundly human, this ability to love so deeply, so intensely, that the absence of that one person carves out caverns of grief within us? Love doesn't promise immunity from grief. In fact, it guarantees it. But there is a strange kind of depth and beauty in this certainty, a poignant grace in this vulnerability...

And so, we grieve. Because we loved. Because we love still. Grief, in essence, is Love in another form. The raw wound of grief, though painful, is also transformative. As it heals, a deeper understanding of love unfolds. We realize that love doesn't die with the absence of another person, doesn't end with goodbyes. It simply transforms, finds a new rhythm, a new way of existing within us.

Love, like water, adapts to its vessel, shaping itself to our experiences, our emotions, our trials and tribulations. So too does grief shape itself within us. As we process, as we heal, it sculpts new chambers within our hearts. These chambers are not filled with emptiness or loss, but rather with enduring affection, with resilience, with wisdom. This wisdom, borne of heartache, illuminates a path forward, not away from love, but deeper into its grasp.

Grief, then, becomes a catalyst for growth, for evolution. It invites us to revisit the depths of our capacity to love, to expand it, to understand its nuances better. It's a way into the very heart of what makes us human - our ability to feel deeply, to love profoundly, and to carry on, changed yet enriched by the experience.

The physical absence of a loved one doesn't take away love; it merely changes its melody. The song continues, woven with notes of remembrance, resilience, and an enduring symphony of love that plays on, forever undying, forever resonating within us.

We love, we grieve, and in that dance, we discover what it means to be human. We find strength, resilience, and compassion in the quiet companionship of our shared experiences, and in that discovery, we learn a little more about love, about grief, and about ourselves.

Imagine Love

Imagine a Love,
a love so profound,
unanchored, unmeasured, with no bound.
A radiant warmth,
a relentless tide,
an embrace from which you cannot hide.

Imagine a Love,
a nourishing rain that asks for nothing,
embraces all,
the joy and pain.
It seeks no return,
no debt to be paid,
in its soft radiant light,
all shadows fade.

Imagine a Love,
so vast, so deep,
it's the promise
that the universe silently keeps,
it cradles your essence,
in waking and sleep,
it's the secret within us that quietly seeps.

This Love doesn't bargain,
doesn't keep score,
it loves you in silence,
forevermore.
It bathes you in grace,
through your very core,
it's a love that's both
the ocean and the shore.

Imagine a Love,
constant as the stars,
beyond the constructs
of our earthly bars.
It's the hidden fabric
that binds near and far,
in its gentle hands,
you're the guiding star.

This Love
is you,
it's me,
it's all,
it is
in the rise
and in the fall,
it's the whispered answer to our soul's call,
it's the thread that connects us,
through the great and the small.

In this Love,
we find our way,
from the edge of night to the break of day.
It's the silent symphony in which we play,
in its sacred rhythm, as one we sway.

In this Love,
there's no You or I,
there's only the breath of the endless sky.
It's the state of being where we meld,
it's the gateway to the Oneness,
in its depths, we are upheld.

Unconditional Love,
both the question and reply,
in the eternal moment, where we align.
The pure essence of us, where secrets lie,
the home within, is where we unify.

A Potter's Touch

Upon the wheel that spins the days,
Life's potter molds our earthen ways.
A vessel formed with tender care
through joy and strife, a Life we share.

Each touch a guide, our path unfolds,
in artful balance life's dance molds,
a subtle force, the hands of fate
transform the clay, as we create.

The spiral dance, our hearts connect,
in joy and pain our lives reflect,
as cycles turn, emotions sway,
a masterpiece of life's display.

Let's twirl and sway on this life's stage,
in each graceful spin, let's truly engage.
Embrace the spin of life's potter's wheel.
in every turn, our souls reveal.

A Grace We Come to Know

Love is
the heartbeat,
the deepest trance,
the pulse in life's expansive, ever-spinning dance.
Untamed, out of control,
no set or predetermined stance,
within its boundless endless expanse,
we live, we breathe in Love's romance.

We can't harness a heart,
seal feelings or stake a claim,
yet, in Love, we can remain,
we can deeply feel and embody Love,
ethereal and real,
and for Love's touch,
we can appeal...

Bathed in its essence,
we come alive,
through acts of Love,
we truly thrive.

We are Love
if we fall losing control,
in Love's chaos
we become whole.

To love is
to be a spark in the dark,
a joy in despair,
a flame amidst the cold,
a gentle glow in shadow's way..

To be loved,
a grace we come to know...

Eternal Echo

In my quiet stillness, in the sting of my grief,
when loss feels vast beyond belief,
I bring this thought to get relief:
Love never dies, it always flows, it's not a thief.
I take a breath...
And I repeat...

It may seem that love has slipped away,
leaving echoes of words left unsaid,
but love is not lost when tears are shed,
it's the pulse within, life's connecting thread...

Love isn't tied to the form we wear,
it braves the storm, its essence ever clear,
even through the gloomiest of haze,
Love is the light that always remains.

So, I behold in my heart all the moments shared,
laughter, the dreams that I dared,
Love's echo in memories aired,
became solace in the midst of grief's despair.

I'm allowing the tears, letting my heart weep,
in love's endless depth, I steep.

Falling

There's a surrender in the falling...
a quiet letting go,
not a calculated calling,
but a river's gentle flow.

I didn't choose the falling,
it came as the softest blow,
just like a silent snowflakes' calling,
covering the world below.

There's a mystery in the falling,
a secret only the heart can know
in the silence of moonlight's calling,
underneath the starlight's glow.

There's an immersion in the falling,
where the deepest currents flow,
Love, not a shallow sprawling,
but an ocean deep below.

The falling...
it's not a journey,
or a path we consciously sow;
it's more like a dance, silently swirling,
a rhythm innate, as time continues to flow.

In falling,
I touch my essence,
in between the give and take,
the rise and fall,
in the heart's tender epicenter,
where love freely grows.

So, here,
in the truth of falling,
where fears are laid low,
In Love,
I came to know...

GENUINE THRUM OF LOVE

Yes, I thought about Love today... Not just that butterflies-in-your-stomach kind of feeling, but the one that's deep, bare-your-soul kind of love. The kind that's about more than just you or me—it's about us; and not just us, but everyone. That we're all in this together, bound by this invisible thread of Love.

This Love... a love that goes beyond just feelings—more than a heart skipping a beat or a fleeting rush of warmth. It's the kind of love that truly wishes for another's well-being without expecting anything in return. Sounds grand, doesn't it? Yet, we've all had a taste of this love in one way or another, in our unique experiences and connections.

When this love blossoms, it doesn't recognize boundaries. It blurs the lines between 'you' and 'I', turning strangers into family, making the world a little smaller and a lot warmer. It's a love that humbles us, that shows we're not so different after all.

This Love, at its core, is the heartbeat of Life. It's the unseen force that turns ordinary moments into extraordinary memories. When we love like this—when we let ourselves truly feel—we are being our most authentic selves. Unfiltered. Real. Raw. Honest.

Bare Hearts

In every heartbeat's tender thrum,
lies a narrative of love, from where we've come.
Not a fleeting emotion, peddled or sold,
but Love—it's us, raw, unrefined, and whole.

Love
is a symphony played on the strings of mankind,
no score is kept, no debts to bind,
just a wish for your ease, no strings to unset.
It sees us intertwined, in this vast scheme,
as a single stroke in life's vibrant dream.

Love,
is where the Ego melts like ice in the sun,
in love's glow, the illusion is undone,
'You' and 'I',
once lines in the sand,
blur in the wash of love's gentle hand.

Love?
It's the pulse of our shared existence,
the constant hum in the background of persistence.
It's not a spectacle, not a grand event,
but a quiet acceptance, in a gentle descent.

Love,
it's no orchestrated dance,
but the soul's raw rhythm in its purest stance.

Love is not a chore,
not a mask to wear,
but the authentic voice,
that dares to bare.

So...
    Love,
isn't a rehearsed play,
it's the sun's warm kiss on a cold winter's day.
Love is not a pretense,
nor a practiced art,
but the sincere song,
of a candid heart.

...and yet again, today, I thought about Love...
Love isn't just something we do, it's what we are
at our core. Love is as essential to us as breathing,
and just as natural. Forgetting that, we might lose
touch with a part of our humanity that's truly
worth cherishing...

Universal Love

Universal Love, a force so grand,
it flows through every grain of sand,
it's not a thing that can be bought or sold,
but rather, it's an energy to behold.

In every creature, great and small,
it's the pulse, that beats within us all,
it's the beauty that surrounds us here,
from the stars above to the Earth, so dear,

it's the gentle breeze and the morning light,
a wondrous symphony that fills the night,
it's the force that connects us all,
from the tiniest creature to the great and tall.

It transcends all borders and divides,
in its warm embrace, every soul thrives.
It's the light that guides us through the dark,
a ray of hope, a vibrant spark;

It's the music that fills our hearts,
a symphony of life that never departs;
It's the whisper in the gentle breeze,
and the rustle of the autumn leaves;

It's the warmth of the sun on your skin,
and the coolness of the rain as it begins;

It's the smile on a stranger's face,
and a tender loving embrace.

As Universe is Love and always here,
guiding us through every joy and tear,
So, I open up my heart and let it flow,
in Universal Love, I am forever whole.

Through the Looking Glass of the Soul

Through eyes that see the world around,
pure reflections to be found,
because all we see is but a view
of our own selves in a subtle hue.

It's not the thing before our sight
that makes our vision pure and bright,
but rather, what we carry in,
that shapes the world that we begin.

So if we see with hearts of hate,
we'll find in others that same trait,
and miss the beauty all around
in every sight, in every sound;

But if we look with eyes of Love,
we'll find our souls expand above and beyond,
and in each moment, we'll ever find,
the magic of life, through love's design.

All I see is but a glimpse
of what within my being imprints,
and in this way, I come to see
that I'm the one who sets me free.

So I choose my lenses well,
and with each view, my soul compels
to seek the good, the true, the kind,
and leave the shadows far behind.

Because all you see is but a reflection,
of your soul's own direction;
and in this way, we come to find
our truest selves,
                    our purest mind...

Healing Rhythm

In the silent hours when my laughter fades to a sigh,
and the world feels as vast and distant as the midnight sky,
when heartache paints my dreams in melancholic hues of blues,
I remember, life still sings in heart-stirring views.

I witness daisies in the garden greeting the day
so bold and bright,
bathing under the tender veil of the soft morning light.
In their fragile resilience, I find a hopeful cue,
life's rhythm carries on, pure and true.

Does the hummingbird halt its fluttering delight,
when the garden's colors surrender to the cool arms of night?
No, it dances in the dawn's renewing dew,
embracing each moment, as if it's brand-new.

I, just like seasons, know winter's chill,
yet also the promise of spring's thrill
on a seemingly distant hill...
In the relentless pulse of life, one truth rings clear:
with love's compassionate touch,
there's nothing left to fear.

Love is the golden light that breaks the darkest night,
it's the artist that paints the dawn with strokes of warm sunlight;
it's a bridge, sturdy and strong, leading from the familiar known
into the arms of tomorrow's promises shown.

Love is the hidden giggle amidst the tears,
the courageous whisper that quells mounting fears,
it's the memory held close, a comforting reprise,
a glimmer of joy dancing in the stormy skies.

So, when the world feels cold and overwhelmingly vast,
I look to love's warmth, unsurpassed.
Through joy and sorrow, whatever comes my way,
in every fleeting moment, I'm letting Love sway,
feeling its rhythm...
tender, healing, and true,
where every sorrow's etched,
love's solace engraves its clue.

Interlaced

Almost dawn...
Still half-asleep among sheets,
tucked in bed.
A conversation happening...
in my head:

I love talking to you...
Interlaced...
It's like flying through an absolutely untamed, unpredict-
able, freely flickering conversational space.
From the ocean's pulse to the tea leaf's steep,
words find their form with a natural sweep,
and stories spun,
they're so swift,
so easy...
feels sweet...
do not quit, I just want to keep following...
keep tracing...
the experience so deep...

For those who say love's found in tears,
who dig through sorrow, year by year...
I've trodden that path, and this I know—
Love isn't bound to the dark depths below.
It's a myth that love rewards your scars,
though, yes,
it too lives where tears are stars.

So if you search the ocean for what's freely in air,
just to discover love lives both here and there,
Love's not confined to tear-streaked goodbyes,
or the spark on the surface of playful eyes,
it's in the scent of a midnight bloom,
and the silent corners of an empty room,
it's in a laugh,
a glance,
a simple touch,
in quiet moments that say so much.

A chicken and an egg—a consequence and a beginning.
Those consumed by suffering,
dull their other feelings,
those attached to hurt—a feedback loop,
see their lives tinged in dark hue
when the switch goes off as they realize
how unbearably bitter became their blood streaming
through veins,
thrumming in their heart...
But it can be different,
you know,
and it's why your tears so freely flow...
Because bathed in the light of your glowing smile,
all is beautiful—mundane becomes divine.

Why,
please, why do we twist and twine,
complicating matters all the time?

There are plenty of pathways to fleeting divine—
178 thousand ways for Joy to align,
and when those ways fade out,
from the void, a new measuring system takes stage
fueling our endless chase
on the path we trace in this hectic maze
searches for heroes, for skies to graze,
looking to be saviors in celestial sights,
to scale new peaks, discover new lights,..
And this is fine...
This quest is fair, it's not misplaced—
yet let's not erase the need for a harbor,
for some breathing space.

The world smiles, squints through the clouds—
peering at you with adoring eyes,
recognizing the luminescence you are,
and the way you love...
so openly
that it's seemingly easy to destroy you with a single match,
because it's like leaving the gas tank open,
knowing how easy it is for someone to throw the match
into the blaze of an open heart...
A struck match,
a burst of light—
yet you'll see the flame only dances, nurtures, gives life.
Unquenchable,
even when touched by another's spark,
it grows, spreads, dispelling the dark.

Understand,
though it seems easy to destroy you,
in reality,
your love's blaze is what sees you through.
Because every act, every thought, every compassioned plea,
is not just possible but unstoppable because of this Love,
you see...
within those who scream, you recognize children—
children wounded somewhere, somehow, by someone,
carrying invisible scars, carved by hands unknown...
you see...
how they shield themselves in windowless rooms,
so this virus of love can't reach them...
I remember...
I've been there...
I know...
the air there is still and musky...
hard to breathe...
So let's get out,
go for a walk,
let the fresh air fill your lungs once more
so you can see...
It is allowed to be open,
to be true,
it's ok.
It feels good
to open up,
to open your shoulders, open smile, open heart...

It is important to be genuine in suffering and pain, yet...

it feels good to be a sincere open glow
in joy and happiness,
It seems like authenticity is missing in today's artificial
world, walling before our eyes, dividing, compartmentaliz-
ing, isolating....
But, the world can be warm,
even if the skies are shut tight with lazy clouds...
because there, below,
everyone who carries a virus of the Sun, letting the glow out,
sharing it,
warming others around...
and that's how happiness comes and stays...
and that's what we do...

Ok, enough lying in bed, time to get up,
what sleep are you talking about?...
the shivers all over your skin...
and there is no point in understanding something...
or anything...
If only a sincere, genuine hug from the depth of my soul I
could give you,
your soul would sing a song of a boundless sea all day,
or maybe a week,
or maybe all three...

and I roll on my side...
Yet again, my core I touched...
and if I wouldn't touch it, I think I would lose my mind, or
myself for this matter...
or maybe...

I would find it...
again...

In the Heartland of Love

In the heartland of Love,
I crafted my dreams,
Cityscapes of hope,
stitched with golden seams.

Then life unfolded, not at all as planned,
an echo rebounded
through the chambers of my heart,
while I watched my dream shatter,
ripping a wound apart.
Our shared laughter,
our shared truth,
slipped away,
as I stood shivering alone,
engulfed by a cold, rainy day...

Every smile, every laugh, etched in my soul,
suddenly absent, left a gaping hole,
a space filled with fear and despair,
shadowed in sorrow,
nights that stole comfort,
dread of tomorrow...

A piece of me lost, my identity stripped,
a sense of completeness, now abruptly ripped.
In the mirror, a stranger's gaze returns,
watching life that's been flipped and overturned.

Yet within this grief a subtle art I found,
a dance with pain, profound exploration, internally
bound.
I could rush for relief, claim a new dream,
but instead, I've learned to let sorrow stream...

Grief floods in a relentless tide;
The mind's futile struggle, a desperate, lonely ride.
A frantic grab for anything, for a solid hold,
yet, healing requires patience and love to uphold.

So I tread lightly in the fog of despair,
Not fleeing, nor chasing, just being aware.
Aching for solace, longing for release,
in the depth of silence, I found my peace...

Grief wasn't my enemy, nor a curse from above,
but a testament to my endurance,
a testament to my Love,
a Love that won't die.

The dream may have died,
faded from sight into the deep night,
but I, the dreamer, persisted towards the light,
a new way of being,
tender and wide
I found
after my dream had died.

With patience,
I braved through the storm's fierce tear,
humbled by loss,
by love,
by fear...

Then slowly,
ever so slowly,
the raw edges mended,
and in the quiet,
a sense of peace descended.

Timidly,
I stepped into a new sphere,
where new dreams whispered,
promising to appear.
Yet these dreams are different,
still to be sown,
blooming from loss,
from Love,
from the strength I've grown.

THE STORY OF A GRIEVING HEART

Grief is a deeply personal, often overwhelming emotion that touches us in ways that words can hardly capture. It lingers in the hidden corners of your heart, whispering in the quiet spaces left behind by what we have lost. Each loss is unique; each ache is a distinct shade of sorrow, resonating with a pain that is profoundly your own.

Yet, in the midst of this intimate pain, there is a connection that binds us all. Our individual stories of grief may differ in circumstance and detail, but the core emotion, the very essence of loss and longing, is a shared human experience. Whether it's the grief of a lost loved one, the end of a cherished relationship, a dream unfulfilled, or a place left behind—these are not just personal tales; they are the universal echoes of the human heart.

And it's in these very personal and intimate stories that we find a connection, a shared experience. It's the story of a Grieving Heart, and it's a tale as old as humanity itself.

It's about Love—the kind that doesn't fade with the softest whispers of goodbye, or with dreams that slip through our fingers like strands of morning mist. It's a love that exists in letting go, as much as in the joy of holding close. This is the love that sits with us in the silence, unwavering, as we navigate the spaces that our losses leave behind. It's the love found in the well-worn edges of a photograph, in the steadfast pulse of memory, in the quiet courage to face another day.

This love is the silent companion to our sorrow, the warmth that coexists with the cold emptiness of absence. It's the love that endures, not just in the joyous clasp of hands or the resonance of laughter shared but also in the quietest moments when the heart aches. It's the light that remains when the stars of our hopes seem to dim, a gentle affirmation that even in the act of letting go, we hold on to what matters most.

Pure love, then, is this truth—that it remains through the trials of change, a touchstone in the midst of our personal tempests, a testament to the connections that bind us beyond time, beyond words, beyond presence. Such love doesn't fade; it transforms into the quiet resilience that underscores our grief.

In the heart of it all, there is a singular truth: the more we love, the more we grieve. They are two sides of the same precious coin. You cannot truly understand one without embracing the other. Grief is not the absence of love, but its reflection, its consequence, its testimony.

Our individual stories may be different, filled with unique experiences and emotions, but they all lead us to the same place—to a recognition of what it means to be human, to love, and to lose. It is not a journey of isolation but of empathy and connection.

This is not merely my story; it's ours. It's the story of One Grieving Heart, echoing through the ages, resonating in each of us, bridging our differences, and reminding us that in our loss, in our pain, in our longing, we are never truly alone.

And in this shared narrative, we find not only solace but also an understanding, a validation of our human experience, that in our vulnerability, in our authenticity, in our grief, we find our strength, our compassion, our love.

This is the story of a Grieving Heart. The story of Love. It's our story.

In spaces between breaths I find,
an uncharted world, a quiet mind,
a reckoning pure, a self so true,
a hidden path that leads to renewal.

THE PATH FORWARD

As our time together here withers away, it's not a final parting but a quiet pause in the ongoing journey we share. Should you ever need to revisit these words for comfort or reflection, know that this place remains for you. This isn't an end but a waypoint in your own journey through grief and understanding. This book began as my solitary reflections—words and emotions poured onto pages during moments of profound personal change. Now, these same words mark a path we've walked together.

In these pages, I've invited you into the most personal spaces of my heart and mind. You've witnessed the contours of my grief, the ebbs and flows of pain and healing that are deeply personal, yet universally understood. I shared the core of my story in hopes it would resonate with your own experiences, offering solace, recognition, and a sense of companionship.

Reflecting on this journey, I am struck by the resilience of the human spirit and our capacity for healing. Grief, with its many faces, challenges and changes us, but also connects us in profoundly deep ways. My hope is that these words have served as a bridge between my heart and yours, and between all who find themselves navigating the unpredictable waters of loss.

As you move forward, carrying your own stories and experiences, may you find comfort in the power of shared narratives to heal, to connect, and to bring solace. May the words of this book not just linger as a reminder of sorrow, but stand as a testament to the strength, hope, and love that remain even in our darkest hours.

I hope you carry with you not just my words, but the connections they forge and the understanding they impart. May they remind you that grief is not an isolated experience, but a shared human condition that binds us in our fragility and our strength.

In sharing my heart, my grief, and my reflections, I have found solace, and I hope you have too. Thank you for embracing my story and allowing it to become a part of yours.

May we all continue to find beauty in the broken, strength in the sorrow, and grace in the grief.

Be Alive,
Love, Julia

LA DELANEY

300

A Meeting Point

A line set free, a thought expressed,
in solitude, it left my chest,
yet somewhere on a distant shore,
it found a heart, a kindred soul,
a stranger...
yet a hidden whole,
in words and whispers, I could trace,
a shared embrace in timeless space.

No words returned, no voice to hear,
yet deep within, the truth was clear,
a quiet hum,
a gentle touch,
my words had meant...
had meant so much...

A glance,
a smile across the page,
a meeting point is a silent stage...

The words, once mine, now freely soared,
a connection made, in Life's loving core.

Stay connected with me at PositivePranic.com for an extension of our shared exploration into healing and hope.

positivepranic.com

Step into a space where my poetry and prose extend the comfort and understanding you found in these pages. Discover resources and free guided meditations crafted to accompany you on your journey—offering a pause for reflection and a breath of serenity.

My writer's story:

positivepranic.com/uncharted

And if this book has touched you, please consider sharing your experience with others. Your review could greatly help and deepen our collective understanding of grief.

Your honest thoughts and reflections are invaluable. I am deeply grateful for every word shared. Your voice matters—both to me and to those walking this similar path.

Made in United States
Troutdale, OR
05/13/2024

19839278R00190